EMBRACE THE UNKNOWN

WITH

CERTAINTY

Marianne Parent LMHC, MA

*Developing a peaceful friendship with the realities of **CHANGE** and **UNCERTAINTY** is a life long process.*

ISBN Number: 9781980893943

I am reborn each day
I wake up to a new life
A new day
New experience
It is a fresh day
No past attached

I am reborn today and everyday. Being reborn each day means all options – all opportunities are mine to experience – have – feel grateful – feel joy – laughter – release – relief. In the new day I have MISSED OUT ON NOTHING because the past does not exist in the new day. Only NOW opportunities – NO past energy of anger, resentment or regret – only NOW EXPERIENCES.

(Inherent Value)

DEDICATION

Mom and Dad who loved me first and always.

To every client, YOUR energy helped create this book.

STOP TRYING TO FIX YOURSELF.

YOU ARE NOT BROKEN.

"FIX ME FATIGUE" WILL SET IN.

YOU ARE A HUMAN BEING WITH GIFTS AND FLAWS.

ENJOY YOUR LIFE WHILE SEEKING OPPORTUNITIES TO LEARN.

(Corrective Experience)

Only YOU can expand your level of
EMOTIONAL MATURITY.

Endlessly looking for someone else to fulfill this role is impossible.

No one else can do YOUR emotional internal work, because no one else knows what is best for YOU.

You alone have access to your **INTERNAL WISDOM**, *and only* **YOU** *can apply it to your life.*

Trusting yourself and building your life one choice and decision at a time is your work.

(Corrective Experience)

Contents
Part I

Part II

Part III

*Use **YOUR** past as a stepping stone to learn and move towards **YOUR LIFE**. When you LEARN from the past and use it as a stepping stone, you psychologically turn the past into a positive, because you are using what you have learned to **BENEFIT** yourself in the present day.*

(Corrective Experience)

*When you are numbing your emotions, you block access to your **INTERNAL WISDOM**, and wonder why you experience a void and feel so painfully alone in your life.*

(Inherent Value)

1

EMBRACE THE UNKNOWN WITH CERTAINTY

"EMBRACE THE UNKNOWN WITH CERTAINTY" is a statement of INTERNAL WISDOM revealed at a point of emotional and physical exhaustion. I needed to make a drastic change. I was terrified to take an ACTION STEP to change because it went against my overly responsible personality. I trusted the wisdom and made the most amazing discovery within myself.

My INTERNAL WISDOM unexpectedly spoke to me one night. I woke up that morning one person and literally went to bed a changed person. I was different in how I began to view my life and emotionally live in the world to this day. The dramatic change came through discovering a belief I was not consciously aware of having, and realizing how this unconscious belief was impacting my life. Beliefs are very powerful indeed.

I OVERGAVE to my family, my friends, and my work. Eventually, an increase in medical issues resulted in needing several surgeries. I began a meditation and writing practice to help deal with the stress This type of writing is fast and flowing with no concern for punctuation or spelling. This type of writing bypasses the conscious mind and reaches INTERNAL WISDOM.

Following several surgeries I concluded I would need to resign from my job to regain my physical, emotional, and spiritual health. I have worked since the age of fifteen and have been overly responsible most of my life (Overgiving). Resigning my position with no guaranteed job waiting for me, and needing to pay my own bills seemed an impossible leap to take. One day while sitting on the couch of my dear friend, Jan, I took a small step in the direction of following the guidance of my INTERNAL WISDOM. I stated to Jan that I did plan to leave my job as a therapist to give myself the gift of three months away from work to only take care of myself. My willingness to state this out loud and make a CHOICE only for myself started my creative energy moving in the direction of how to make this happen.

Over the next year I saved money. My conviction to resign my position and ONLY take care of myself grew stronger and stronger. Yet, life can be ironic in how it tests our commitment to make changes. The very week I planned to give my notice at work and felt ready to take the leap by trusting MYSELF and MY INTERNAL WISDOM, the stock market crashed. I lost a great deal of my retirement investments and savings. Jobs became very scarce. This was somewhat of an emotional set back (Worry Habit)!

To resign my job now and leave everything I had known, especially my HABIT of being an overly responsible person, would go against almost every decision I had ever made in my life. When my fear and anxiety from second guessing the sanity of my decision was at an all time high, I was sitting in my daily meditation. I opened my eyes, picked up my pen and wrote, "EMBRACE THE UNKNOWN WITH CERTAINTY." I knew at that moment I would take the leap. My willingness to take this leap provided so many gifts. The life changing emotional gift was that I was able to resolve feelings I had secretly been struggling with since childhood; "Why did I often feel so sad, and feel that I was not the one supposed to be here."

I had experienced a profound sense of sadness my entire life. I could never understand why, because my actual life in no way reflected these feelings. I was never able to identify where these intense feeling of sadness were originating from in my life. I had a good life, wonderful parents and knew I was loved. Why did I always feel an overwhelming sense of sadness and grief as a child, when my life in no way reflected these intense and persistent feelings? The answer came fifteen days into my "sabbatical" and changed how I would emotionally experience my life forever.

I gave my notice in February despite my fears and the anxiety of others in my life. I decided for the first time to live each day with no plan, no agenda other than taking care of ME. This was a very new experience as I had taken care of other people my entire life, often putting myself last. I planned to take three months off. However, this extended into nine months. Up to that point in my life I always needed a plan and agenda. Thankfully, I have learned having NO agenda and NO plan is a much more peaceful path for me.

Three days into my time off, I was looking out my window at the snow and felt paralyzed with fear that I had made the wrong decision. Although I had taken an ACTION STEP that supported my INTERNAL WISDOM, my fear-filled voices did not remain silent. Some days they were screaming; "What is the matter with you, are you crazy?" "You need to call and get your job back." This CHANGE is a daunting reality, when you are an overly responsible person who just quit her job after the stock market crashed. I continued to repeat my mantra, "EMBRACE THE UNKNOWN WITH CERTAINTY" to help drown my fears.

One evening fifteen days into what I came to call my sabbatical, I was minding my own business quietly reading a book. A specific comment on GRIEF triggered a sudden and unexpected avalanche of emotional energy and subconscious writing to flow. It felt uncontrolled and not of me, but it was me writing the letter. It was my energy and my INTERNAL WISDOM pouring out on the pages. I could not keep up with the pace of the writing as the energy was flowing out so fast. My INTERNAL WISDOM was clear and specific.

I share part of the original letter as it reflects my belief in seeking our INTERNAL WISDOM as a guide and our life-long learning process of trusting it. I have typed the letter as written and have not corrected spelling or punctuation.

My internal voice begins.....

Sadness and happiness met me at birth, trying to fill a role that was not mine. I was born into sadness, not joy - I was there to make up for the loss of a child - I was born to make it better - I wondered why with the good life I had I could not feel the joy of it. I have felt it has been my role to be the child to be born to make up for the child that was lost. My birth was not one of joy for my own spirit coming into the world - it was a replacement for the one that was not able to make it into the world. I know this is not true but my life has reflected this belief - I wonder if people said to my mother that I made up for the one that was lost - the burden of being the child that came next - I am a spiritual being and my lesson in life is learning about saying Goodbye. I was born into my own role - one that begins and ends in JOY - I was born to live a life I needed to live- I am not my sister who died at birth - I was born next but can never make up for the loss - I let it all go to God's healing. I have unconsciously tried my whole life to make up for the loss - I free myself of this - I was born 50 weeks after my mother lost a child - a twin - I was a girl - she was a girl - my birth must have been a time of remembering the loss of her not making it into the world - sadness and happiness met me at birth - I have felt the UNCONSCIOUS BURDEN to make the loss better for my family - it is not my role - I gratefully give this up. There are no bad people, only unresolved grief and sorrow of my mom and dad losing a child - my parents doing the best they could at the time - I must move out of the shadow of my family's past sadness it does not belong to me - never has but now I know where the sadness came from - **I am the child that made up for the loss** - I only TODAY consciously realize I have held this emotional energy all my life until tonight - I cannot accept this role - I must shed it.

(The voice in the writing changes)

For you to have the LIFE I have designed you need to know this - the pain is OK - it is real - cry - give what you give to others to yourself - compassion and empathy for the mistakes with the belief of doing better - continue to sit in the silence - I AM with you -you are not alone-you absorbed the role of the replacement because your family needed you to heal - yet you got stuck in the role of the REPLACEMENT which was not the plan you had for your life. Do not fear or be sad - all you have wanted is coming flooding in - hold on for the ride - get ready for the ride - you are an adult not a child - no one is to blame - I can release myself from a life long role that was not my life plan - It is in the silence that all is known. I am an expression of joy for my own life - sorrow is simply a HABIT - cultivate your true self - End.

Before reading back the twelve page letter I had written, I had no conscious memory of its contents. I felt emotionally disoriented for several days. When I read the letter again, I saw my back and forth struggle between unconscious beliefs I have held since birth, battling with present day conviction that I deserve my own life. The letter reflected the emotional struggle I have experienced my entire life. This struggle vacillated between unconscious beliefs I held, and my TRUE belief in the present day. **I could finally understand why the energy of the present always seemed to be intertwined with another very sad energy.** Only by this revelation did I realize that the sadness did not belong to me. The day after my writing when I woke in the morning, my body was in pain, a throbbing like I had never experienced. My body ached for many days from letting go of the energy of sorrow I had carried. The trapped energy of grief my body had held all of my life finally released.

13

I was not aware my family had suffered this loss until my older sister mentioned it to me one night. I was fifteen then and in high school. I had not been aware my older sister had been a twin until that night. I had felt sad energy since I was a little child YEARS before I had any conscious knowledge of the loss. I could feel the tremendous burden of the grieving energy, but did not know what it was about, or where it was originating from. I never had any CONSCIOUS thought that this loss had any impact on me, because the family loss had happened PRIOR to my being born. I knew with every part of my being the writing answered the question of why the energy of grief, as well as feeling that I was not the one supposed to be here, had always been so present. I remember sitting in a conference on family therapy and the speaker made a comment about what it is like for a child who is born after the loss of a child. He said, "Well the one who comes next has a great burden to bear, because they not only have to live their life, but they have to live the life of the one before."

My life was my own for the first time without the unconscious burden of trying to make up for the loss. That night my entire view of myself and my life had changed. My natural way is to absorb the energy of other people around me. I have always experienced emotions of others very intensely. I experience how others are feeling without them speaking. I feel the energy of their emotions as well as my own. When I was younger I struggled to separate my emotions from the emotions of others. I believe this dynamic contributed to my internalizing the emotions of those around me, when I was conceived approximately three months after the loss. There was never a verbal story to these feeling of grief. I did not experience the loss in words only by absorbing the feeling energy of those around me. I have a sister whose energy I had carried probably since conception. I needed to see we were two different people, two different energies and I wanted to see where she was buried. I needed to say HELLO!

I resolved to find where she was buried and did not know where to start. I found out my older sister may have had some information, so I drove to Maine for a visit. I told her about the writing and she understood the importance of my being able to find the site to visit. She explained the grave was hard to find as the babies fifty years ago had been buried in one part of the cemetery, which now looked like a football field. You would never know what was buried under the grass. Each grave is marked with a number engraved on a small round circle of steel buried under the ground. These silver markers are two feet apart. She had a conference that weekend, but said she would drive down the following weekend and we could go together.

The next day I was driving home from Maine and experienced an intense feeling of energy. I KNEW I did not need to wait for my sister. I KNEW I would find it myself. I arrived home, sat in

14

my meditation, pen and paper ready, and wrote the following; "Sister I need to come and find you - show me how to find you?" I sat in silence for a while and then wrote, "Drive there and walk out to where you think."

The next day I drove to the cemetery and followed the directions my sister had given to find the general area. When I pulled up to the site, it looked exactly as she had described it. It was a huge lawn of grass and seemed to be nothing more. I followed the INTERNAL WISDOM that had come to me in my writing and walked out onto the lawn "to where I thought." I stopped. I thought, well, what do I do know? It popped into my head (Internal Wisdom), my sister had mentioned each grave was marked by a small silver marker buried UNDER the grass. I thought maybe if I could find one small piece of silver in the grass and dig it up I might be able to see how close I was to the site I was seeking. Well, for whatever reason (Internal Wisdom), I took two steps to the right. While looking down I saw a small piece of silver sticking out of the grass, the size of a dime. I bent down and started to dig. The marker I found was number S.V. 83 and my sister is buried in S.V. 84 two feet over. I started to dig two feet to the right and there it was S.V. 84. My sister.

I had walked out onto a lawn the size of a football field, and found my sister's marker buried several inches below the grass in less than ninety seconds (Internal Wisdom). You might think I was shocked. No, I knew I would find it! I stood at the site for a long time. I wrote a little note and buried it in the grass. I felt sadness that my sister did not make it in. I was healed by emotionally feeling that we are two different people, two different energies with two different life plans.

As I stood at the grave I thought I now know why I had taken the terrifying leap to leave my job and jump into the unknown. My INTERNAL WISDOM needed me to be silent and see myself as the one needing my intense focus, instead of taking care of everyone else. I feel compassion for my mother, father and two older sisters who were in the world at the time of this loss. I know they never saw me as a replacement or one that took the place of another. They loved ME for ME. Once the sad energy had a verbal story, I KNEW it was not my experience. Once the unconscious belief was made conscious it had no emotional meaning or influence over me. I was born into my own life. I have my own life. I did not take anyone's place. I have a plant that I bought that day. It is in a favorite pot at my home. It helps to remind me that we are two different energies.

I believe then and continue to believe today that my willingness to take an ACTION STEP demonstrated I was worth taking care of and DESERVED time for myself. This trigged an emotional opening in me where the one answer I needed to know about my life could be made conscious. I was healed of the ongoing sadness locked away as unconscious energy regarding a painful loss that occurred PRIOR to my even being born. I returned to the work I love nine months later. What I learned during those nine months has greatly influenced my work with clients. I had planned to take only three months off, yet the time extended to nine months. I guess I needed nine months to be reborn.

ONLY TODAY

Are you living your moments with your head and thoughts turned to the past? What happened yesterday does not determine what is happening TODAY. I do not have to do penance today by dragging the energy of yesterday into today. There is no punishment due today because of yesterday's choices. I AM not penalized for yesterday, TODAY. The past is nothing, only this NOW moment is anything. I AM not going to allow what happened yesterday to take away from MY JOY TODAY. The way to do this is in YOUR THOUGHTS. What happened yesterday is NOW NOTHING. TODAY is a NOW opportunity. Don't bring yesterday into TODAY. Don't bring tomorrow into TODAY.

SIMPLY LIVE TODAY

(Intention)

*Just enjoy the day. When the **Universe** needs **ME**, the **Universe** will give **ME** the NOD. In the meantime **ENJOY!***

(Internal Wisdom)

2

ENERGY WRITING

Seven years after my sabbatical it "popped" into my head one morning that I would write a book (Internal Wisdom). I have never wanted to write a book. I had no idea what topic I would write about, what I would say, or how to have a book published. I took note of my IMMEDIATE negative THOUGHT CASCADE. "It could never happen." "Do you really want to do all that work?" "Do you want to take the risk of being embarrassed?" I have grown accustomed to my INITIAL human reactive thoughts of FEAR attempting to drown the energy of my INTERNAL WISDOM. **Although I have learned to trust my INTERNAL WISDOM, it does not mean that the negative thoughts become totally silent. I practice NOT reacting to the internal emotional contradictions of my INTERNAL WISDOM and fear.** I don't mind the negative thoughts that usually pop up FIRST. After I acknowledge them as being from MY past, they usually drift off. I notice the fear, say hello, smile and move on to following my INTERNAL WISDOM. I felt the UNIVERSE was again giving me the NOD. This time I was to write a book!

Humans have a natural tendency to want to protect themselves from being injured, especially when it comes to being embarrassed and humiliated. Despite my initial fear-filled thoughts to this guidance, the intensity of the feeling (Internal Wisdom) made it clear I would be writing a book. I set a written INTENTION in my journal for this goal, even when I had no idea what I would be writing about. Shortly after setting the INTENTION, all was made clear on how to arrive at a finished product, and how it would be published. That same week, out of the blue, two clients suggested I write a book about the concepts I teach in group. Once I began the process, several other clients suggested I write a book when they had no idea I was already in the process of writing. One week after setting the INTENTION, a mailing came for an evening class on how to publish a book. The class was being held on a Wednesday evening which "just so happened" to be my day off. I signed up for the class. I left the session knowing how my INTERNAL WISDOM'S book would be published. I say my INTERNAL WISDOM'S book, because I still had no idea what I would be writing about, but I was CERTAIN a book was coming. The energy to write began the next day.

Intense feelings of energy ALWAYS precipitate my writing sessions. The book was created in the same manner as my past writings. I never sit down and say, "Time to write." I had paper and pen everywhere so when a thought came up I wrote it down. The flood gates would open, often for several hours at a time. The energy to write usually came during the middle of the night or when I was driving in my car, so I had to pull over. When the energy to write came, I wrote as fast as I could to keep up with the themes. Over time, the ideas in the book developed. It was interesting for me to see after a writing session, what I was actually writing about, and what was included. I knew the book was done when the energy to write stopped. I have expanded on each theme for clarity. You may notice that my style in speaking and writing is to be clear, direct and to the point. My motivation is not to criticize or find fault, but hopefully offer the opportunity to expand your awareness and experience your own creativity. It is through your experiences that you emotionally own the learning.

You can unknowingly be triggering more suffering and not realize how you are creating it. Common behaviors that have become HABITS can be increasing negative energy and decreasing joyful energy in your daily life. You may look to external factors as being the problem, and believe you need to wait for EXTERNAL situations to change before you can feel better. The themes in this book will help you to identify YOUR behavioral patterns that are causing YOU distress. You can begin to observe yourself, and see how your thoughts and mood are impacting your behavior. You will realize through your EXPERIENCE that it is not the external problem that is the issue, but how you are interpreting the situation that impacts your mood. Expanding your awareness and objectively observing your behavior puts YOU in a position of POWER. Increased self awareness expands your OPTIONS. As you identify behaviors that are destructive, you can transition into the powerful energy of having a CORRECTIVE EXPERIENCE by taking an ACTION STEP.

Do not have anxiety about needing to make any change right away. You are in control to make the decision that is best for you at this moment in time. It is perfect to stay exactly where you are, if you are not ready for an ACTION STEP. Don't start a NEGATIVE THOUGHT CASCADE to punish yourself, if you are not ready for an ACTION STEP. When you respect how you feel NOW, you are demonstrating good self care and self acceptance, which is actually an important ACTION STEP. You have ALREADY moved towards change by respecting YOUR starting point. If you are not at the point of feeling you are ready to take a new ACTION STEP, you can begin by using your imagination. Practicing change in your imagination is very powerful. Rehearsing the change in your imagination feels emotionally safe, because you are in control of the story. The power of your imagination develops a blueprint for positive changes you would like to be experiencing in your life. You begin to emotionally experience change as a possibility. Practice in your imagination for as long as you need. There is no rush or need to try to make up for lost time. Trying to make up for lost time keeps you mentally living in the past, and feeling the negative energy of dissatisfaction and regret. Even when you feel you need to make up for lost time, you are not given twenty-nine hours in the day. You have twenty-four hours TODAY. Set an INTENTION to use this undiscovered twenty-four hours to the best of your ability, without regrets of the past seeping in.

If you block access to your feelings, you lose the connection to your INTERNAL WISDOM. You look to external events or relationships attempting to feel connected to something or someone. Until you reconnect to YOUR feelings, even when they are painful, you will search in vain for the longed for feeling of connection. Use your past as a stepping stone by learning and moving towards YOUR LIFE. **When you learn from the past and use it as a stepping stone, you psychologically turn the past into a positive, because you are using what you have learned to BENEFIT yourself in the present day.** You are no longer feeling a victim to your past. That is why, even if it has been difficult and painful, find YOUR learning and move on. Remember, it is not what others feel you should learn, but what YOU feel is the learning in any situation.

The best way I have found to move on from painful past experiences is to focus on what I have learned, and how can I use this learning to be of help to others. I focus on my learning and bring the knowledge with me to use in the future. This may be as simple as not judging myself or others as harshly as I may have done in the past. When negative thoughts pop in, I remind myself I have learned what I can from the past situation, and refocus my thinking back on GRATITUDE. I usually like to refocus on GRATITUDE in the present day. I leave the pain in the past as it serves no purpose NOW. Focusing on present moment gratitude IMMEDIATELY changes my thoughts and mood. I encourage simplicity in making changes. ALWAYS begin from a place of self compassion as you embark on your journey. Yes, you did read that correctly, SELF COMPASSION. Consider starting from the belief that there is no hole or void to fill in you, only learning and moving towards your life. Keep in mind that starting from a thinking pattern of believing you are "broken" or need to be "fixed" will result in very little opportunity to grow. I encourage you to move forward from a thinking perspective that you are open to learning, making changes and expanding your life. **Experience challenges as an opportunity to learn and make different choices.**

Begin to explore the UNLIMITED OPPORTUNITIES OF UNCERTAINTY. If you hold a PRIMARY BELIEF that UNCERTAINTY is a reason for fear, then emotional hesitation, restriction and stagnation sets in. If you learn to emotionally experience UNCERTAINTY as an UNLIMITED OPPORTUNITY, you approach the future with creative energy. One path will be filled with fear and WORRY HABIT. The other path is filled with whatever you might like to create. It is crucial to recognize that we are ALL traveling on a PATH filled with UNCERTAINTY and CHANGE. **How you emotionally experience UNCERTAINTY and CHANGE is within your control.** The POWER of CHOICE and DECISION is YOURS.

I see my role as a therapist as being a passenger in a car offering suggestions and options. The themes in the book are like a passenger riding with you, as you begin the journey of identifying and trusting your INTERNAL WISDOM. You are in the driver's seat and are free to accept or reject any theme, as not all themes will apply to you. You are driving and in complete control of identifying what themes pertain to you, and when you feel ready you can take a new ACTION STEP towards YOUR goal. Let your INTERNAL WISDOM be your ultimate guide. When you arrive at a new destination, we can celebrate YOUR VICTORY together.

My work as a therapist and this book reflect what I have learned during some of the most challenging times in my life. Sharing this knowledge with you brings meaning and purpose to me. The writings at the beginning of each chapter were written many years before the book, yet the themes are very similar. **When you identify with any of the themes in the book, take heart and realize that you are NOT ALONE in your struggles as a human being.** You have the POWER within yourself to change and expand your life. My hope is that a few of the themes in the book will resonate with you. I hope they will inspire you to explore and learn to trust your INTERNAL WISDOM, but most importantly identify ways YOU may be blocking access to it. I share the themes my clients have found most helpful in making changes in their lives. I continue to learn from each of you. I often hear people say that it is a risk to follow their "gut" (Internal Wisdom). The risk is NOT to follow your gut and ignore it. You are ignoring your guidance system. Listen for your INTERNAL WISDOM. It is speaking all the time. Take the risk. DO NOT SETTLE just so YOUR questions in life can be answered. Enjoy and create in the UNLIMITED ENERGY of ***UNCERTAINTY***.

*Remember the revitalizing energy of **uncertainty** and the **unknown**.*

Uncertainty *is Freedom.*

NO BARRIERS.

GO FOR WHAT YOU WANT.

(Worry Habit)

The UNIVERSE can't do it for me. **I MUST FEEL WORTHY** *to bring on my gifts. These feelings of worth must come from within me. My* **INHERENT VALUE** *is already present and I must live as if I believe it. Interact in the world as though I believe I am worth it. The Universe has gifted me with* **INHERENT VALUE.** *It is my job to believe it and live it. Seeking emotional comfort EXTERNALLY is going on an endless search.* **Seeking emotional comfort INTERNALLY is an immediate homecoming.**

(Inherent Value)

3

INHERENT VALUE

If there were ten new born babies arranged in a circle and I asked you to rate the babies from the most valuable baby to the least valuable baby, how would you answer? Most of us would think this was an odd question. Clearly, all the babies have the same INHERENT VALUE, and to assign a value rating to them would seem absurd. This certainty of feeling we are all born with INHERENT VALUE can unfortunately change over time. When do we begin to assign value to ourselves and one another? When did you start to BELIEVE that you had lost YOUR value or feel others around you had lost their value? How does this change happen? You make choices and decisions based on your primary BELIEFS about yourself. Making decisions from a place of feeling valued or not feeling valued will result in very different decisions.

We experience energy from ONE to another. Never broken. ALWAYS.

The energy of ONE is the energy of the other – the wisdom of ONE is the wisdom of the other – the peace of ONE is the peace of the other – the compassion of ONE is the compassion of the other – the love of ONE is the love of the other.

LOVE - INTERNAL WISDOM - HIGHER POWER - GOD - INTUITION - ONE -MOTHER NATURE - UNIVERSE. I consider all the same LOVE ENERGY no matter what name you are comfortable using.

We can think that our INHERENT VALUE has been lost and suffer due to our BELIEF in brokenness about ourselves – our lives – our world. No break has ever or can ever occur. It is only our BELIEF that makes it feel real, and as a result we needlessly suffer due to our false belief. We can be committed to our false BELIEFS. However BELIEF does not equal TRUTH. TRUTH is TRUTH and never changes, while our BELIEFS about our INHERENT VALUE and our lives can change moment to moment. LOVE ENERGY is NEVER changed despite our limited human BELIEFS. LOVE ENERGY is not impacted by our fear-lack-self hate-addictions-anger– resentment. You suffer when you allow yourself to remain in these destructive energies and BELIEF patterns. As you become aware of your BELIEFS in these limited destructive energies, you can challenge the thoughts and release the flow of your INTERNAL WISDOM.

It is my BELIEF that no one can unblock this energy for you. You blocked access to your INTERNAL WISDOM, usually by believing in fear. You alone have the POWER to release the flow and experience the unlimited energy of your INTERNAL WISDOM. Yes I said, YOUR WISDOM. If you don't know what is best for you, who will? Each life is a journey of self. We live in community and are strengthened by human connection, yet we are born and die ("relocate," as my mother would say) as individuals. The energy we create and give off from birth to death is each person's contribution to the world.

You can be influenced and inspired by other human energy, but you will never find YOUR answers in the wisdom of others. Their wisdom is not YOUR internal wisdom, no matter how good it may sound. You must strive to live from your own energy. The most painful energy I have experienced in my own life, and seen in the lives of my clients is when a person is living on a PATH that is not their own. You will only find dead energy on someone else's PATH, because it is not your creative energy. LIVING FULLY according to someone else's energy is impossible. They can believe their energy is best for you by telling you how to live your life (Overhelping). They do not realize they are only offering you dead energy, however helpful they are trying to be. To deny your own dreams and live according to what others pressure you to be, is the most direct way to an existence of misery. Notice I did not say LIFE, but existence. Expecting SOMEONE ELSE to create your life, so you do not have to take the risk is another sure PATH to misery.

You can internalize layers of negative BELIEF patterns about yourself from people in your life. **People can without knowing it, be passing on THEIR unworthy and "less than" BELIEF patterns and fears about themselves to you.** You can unknowingly internalize the negative feedback as your own. The necessity of unlearning the energy of generations of false and fearful BELIEFS cannot be overstated. Once you are on your own creative PATH, life will remain challenging. However, returning to your true PATH and unblocking the flow of your INTERNAL WISDOM makes the experience of living far more enjoyable. When EXTERNAL people and situations become difficult and challenging, your feelings regarding your INHERENT VALUE remain unchallenged and unchanged. The goal is to be living on your own PATH and have peace about yourself. **Yes, EXTERNAL struggles and pressures will continue, but your INTERNAL feelings, what you know and BELIEVE to be TRUE about yourself, will remain at peace**. Once you experience the creative energy of being on YOUR OWN PATH, no other energy no matter how strong and unrelenting, can re-block your INTERNAL WISDOM from flowing to you.

YOUR PRIMARY BELIEFS about yourself color every second, moment, minute, day, week, month, year, decade of your lifetime. A person who believes in their INHERENT VALUE and a person whose primary BELIEF is being "less than" will emotionally experience the same life events in very different ways. How you experience and interpret the same exact event will be colored by the primary view you hold of yourself. BELIEF in being unworthy or "less than" is simply a BELIEF. This BELIEF has no impact on you, unless YOU choose to give it power. **You have IMMEDIATE ACCESS to your personal power of CHOICE.** Despite what your human self may believe, you came into the world with INHERENT VALUE, you live in the world with INHERENT VALUE and you will relocate from the human experience with INHERENT VALUE. Nothing you have done or has been done to you changes the original energy of INHERENT VALUE. You may not be living up to your INHERENT VALUE, but this does not alter the TRUTH. Your BELIEFS that you are unworthy – unlovable – defective – empty – broken, does not change the truth of YOUR INHERENT VALUE.

We all transition into the world with the same inherent worth/value (remember your beliefs about the babies). The challenge is that you do not always live according to your truth of INHERENT VALUE. A sure sign you have forgotten or lost sight of your INHERENT VALUE is you either overvalue yourself or undervalue yourself. Overvaluing takes the form of thinking patterns such as, "I am better than." Undervaluing takes the form of thoughts such as, "I am less than." Thinking you have more value than other people does not come from a place of strength. It is coming from a place of fear. THINKING ENERGY of "feeling better than" is an overcompensation for fear

27

based beliefs about yourself. Feelings of being "better than" or "less than" are coming from the same internal fear. It is simply demonstrating itself externally with different behaviors. Others may observe your mask of "overconfidence" and think it is genuine, when in reality it is being generated from a belief in your lack of worth. YOU know the truth and it leaves you trying to hide by MANAGING YOUR MESSAGE by keeping up the façade. You are living in constant fear and anxiety that others will find you out. This is an exhausting and painful way to live!

When you are CERTAIN of your INHERENT VALUE there is no emotional need to put yourself on a pedestal. When you have respect for your inherent value and worth, you will no longer need to act out this thinking pattern of being "better than" to temporarily try and feel at peace with yourself. Overvaluing and undervaluing yourself and others does take a lot of work. Keeping this false energy going is contrary to your INHERENT VALUE.

You had INHERENT VALUE as a baby, but you have possibly learned and emotionally carry with you a false BELIEF. This false BELIEF creates a life that reflects a great deal of pain, which can be seen in the frequency of your self inflicted wounds (Self Created Chaos). Your CHOICES and DECISIONS are a reflection of how you truly feel about yourself. People say, "See, I have so many problems in life that PROVES I have no worth." In fact, the self inflicted wounds you have manifested are created by your BELIEFS. Your BELIEFS about yourself make it feel true to you. A human life will always have challenges, but you can cut down on the self inflicted wounds by challenging the distorted and negative BELIEFS about yourself. You will make CHOICES and DECISIONS and act this energy into your life according to your primary BELIEFS about yourself. Instead of wasting energy by overvaluing or undervaluing yourself, why not simply VALUE yourself. **Demonstrate this by the CHOICES and DECISIONS you make TODAY.**

I encourage my clients not to work on seeking external energy or getting the outside STUFF. Your external world is reflecting your true beliefs about your self, and your inner belief system about YOUR VALUE. I often hear, "I have achieved so much and have all this STUFF, why don't I feel better about myself?" You mistakenly thought getting external STUFF would quiet the self critical voice of feeling "less than." You are motivated and work hard to achieve external things like money, status, cars and prestige hoping these things will help you prove your value. The result is like rubbing salt in an open wound when this does not happen. You don't know where to go next to feel relief. After years of trying and failing to feel at peace with yourself, FIX ME FATIGUE sets in.

A major road block to learning and making changes is what I like to call FIX ME FATIGUE. You tirelessly have worked for years, sometimes a life time to fix yourself. People spend years of their lives and so much wasted emotional energy trying to FIX IN THEMSELVES WHAT THEY FEEL IS BROKEN. Because you have INHERENT VALUE, you have tried and tried without success to "un-break" in you what has never been broken. Yes, we all have learning and needed changes to work towards, but a common thinking pattern that keeps you stagnant is, "If I could just fix _____ (fill in the blank) in myself I could be happy and enjoy my life." Holding this thinking pattern leads down a despairing path. Why is this path despairing? **When you BELIEVE you need to FIX YOURSELF before you are ALLOWED to enjoy your life, you are basically missing your life.**

FIX ME FATIGUE sets in when your first thought each day is, "What needs to be fixed about me today." Eventually, you lose hope. Human beings will ALWAYS have challenges to work through, so humans never ARRIVE at perfection. I have worked with people who have struggled for their entire lives feeling, "I need to be fixed." They live in sadness, and at times despair that with all their effort, they have never lived at peace within themselves. They feel the time and emotional energy they have expended to FIX themselves has been wasted. They resign themselves to not being able to make any changes, and surrender to a life of not living up to their potential.

FIX ME FATIGUE can lead to actively seeking out ways to EXTERNALLY "FIX" what you feel is broken in yourself. When you emotionally experience your life from this FALSE BELIEF, you seek out EXTERNAL ways to match how you feel and wonder why you keep creating the same results (Self Created Chaos). The problem is that you are starting from the false belief of being "less than" or not good enough. It's that small voice in the back of your head re-playing YOUR, "I am less than" tape that is the problem, not that you have lost your INHERENT VALUE. **You have focused on yourself as a project that needs to be FIXED, rather than a human being with gifts and flaws, who can never lose their INHERENT VALUE.**

Honoring your INHERENT VALUE will quiet the voices, because you are accepting the truth about yourself. You came into the world with INHERENT VALUE and no STUFF. You will "relocate" from the world with INHERENT VALUE and will be leaving all your STUFF behind. Why focus so hard on getting the STUFF? It is not that having success and material STUFF is bad. It is simply that it will never, and can never offer you the experience of living in a peaceful place of feeling your INHERENT VALUE. A quick fix of something external to temporarily distract you may feel good for a moment, yet it is fleeting. When it passes, what remains is YOUR PRIMARY BELIEFS ABOUT YOURSELF, positive and negative. **Your PRIMARY BELIEFS**

about yourself color every second-moment-minute-day-week-month-year-decade of your lifetime.

I cannot recommend strongly enough: **STOP TRYING TO FIX YOURSELF. YOU ARE NOT BROKEN. FIX ME FATIGUE WILL SET IN. YOU ARE A HUMAN BEING WITH GIFTS AND FLAWS. ENJOY YOUR LIFE WHILE SEEKING OPPORTUNITIES TO LEARN.**

1. Do you believe you had INHERENT VALUE when you were born?

2. Can you lose your INHERENT VALUE as a human being? If yes, at what age do you believe you lost your INHERENT VALUE and why?

3. Can your INHERENT VALUE be taken away by others?

4. List five PRIMARY BELIEFS about yourself.

5. How are your PRIMARY BELIEFS impacting what you are creating in your life?

6. How are your PRIMARY BELIEFS impacting your physical health?

I *realize it matters less how my life began.*

What matters most is what I am creating NOW. *I hope to continue creating until it*

*is my time to relocate. I continue to trip, but do my best to learn from the stumble. To the best of my ability **I INTEND** to finish up strong.*

*I believe this can only happen for me if I keep on my **OWN PATH**. A path that begins and ends with continued acceptance of my **INHERENT VALUE**, and of course following the energy of my **INTERNAL WISDOM**.*
(Inherent Value)

If you are regurgitating YOUR past all the time, you will be sick in the present.

(Compassion or Judgment)

4

INTENTION

Hold yourself accountable by setting an INTENTION. Intentions set the goals and standards for YOUR life. YOUR INTENTIONS demonstrate the power you have of creating how you want to feel about yourself. Setting an intention generates energy in the direction you want to be headed. Consistently matching your CHOICES and DECISIONS to your INTENTIONS creates the changes you want to manifest in your life.

Set an INTENTION for what you WANT, not for what you can't have. When you tell yourself, "I can't" your emotional reaction can be to become angry as though you are missing out on something. You nullify your POWER of choice by saying, "I can't" as though you are a victim, and something is being taken away from you.

Setting an INTENTION for an outcome you WANT generates the BELIEF that you will be GAINING something. Imagine if you set an intention to stay on a budget, and you just happen to come across a dress/golf club that you feel you cannot live without. The thought pattern, "I can't buy it" triggers an emotional feeling of loss or missing out. None of us like to feel we are losing. You want to numb the feeling of missing out and attempt to regain emotional control by saying, "I can do what I want." You DECIDE to buy "the stuff" for the quick fix, which ultimately worsens your pain. You gained the EXTERNAL "stuff" at a LOSS of INTERNAL self respect and disappointment with yourself for not keeping your INTENTION. Is having the quick fix (gain) of external "stuff" worth the INTERNAL LOSS of self respect?

When someone says to me, "I can't" buy the dress/golf club I respond by saying, well you can actually buy it. You can go and buy whatever you want. When you say, "I can't" that is not true. You can get up from my office and go shopping right now. I encourage you to say instead, "I AM CHOOSING " not to buy the dress/golf club because of how I want to feel about myself. When you CHOOSE to honor YOUR INTENTION by staying on YOUR budget, you experience the power YOU have to create how you ultimately feel about yourself. **YOUR DECISION translates into the emotional experience of GAINING.** (We all love to feel we are GAINING, unless of course gaining has to do with weight!)

Motivation to make changes to please other people is an emotional set up for failure. You may look to other people as an initial motivation for change, yet setting an INTENTION for what YOU desire is crucial. When stress hits and you want to return to some past comforting behavior (drink-drug-food), you can begin to resent the exact people who were originally motivating you to make changes. You begin to feel they are getting in the way of what you want. Acting on the behavior is more likely because you were not making the change for you. You experience your, "I can't" as being penalized or punished. You again feel loss and disappointment.

When YOU commit to keeping YOUR INTENTION for something you desire, you are more motivated to live up to your own standards. You emotionally experience achieving an outcome YOU DESIRE. **You are changing your emotional experience from losing to GAINING, and will be much more motivated to continue with the new behavior.** CHOOSING to honor YOUR INTENTIONS by taking a new ACTION STEP develops a pattern of self care. By taking care of yourself, YOU emotionally experience feeling in control and creating what you desire in your life.

Do not have one moment of concern about what other people think about you, your dreams or your INTENTIONS. You need to outgrow the adolescent maturity level of looking to your peers or parents to determine how you see yourself, or how you plan to live your life. Their thoughts are not creating your life. **YOUR thoughts are creating your life.** People will spend years of their lives PAINFULLY concerned about what others may be thinking about them, and trying to gain their approval. Depending on how old you are, you probably have figured out that temporarily gaining EXTERNAL approval does not change your life, or change how you feel about yourself.

Other than giving you a TEMPORARY respite from your "less than" voice, other people's approval is fleeting.

I encourage you to take five to ten minutes in the morning and set an INTENTION each day. Developing a routine of taking a few minutes of self care by setting an INTENTION is a powerful way to start the day. You may read something inspirational and motivating, or sit for a few minutes noticing your breath. Ask your INTERNAL WISDOM what will be best for you. Set an INTENTION that reflects what you want the day to emotionally feel like. Frame the INTENTION from the viewpoint of what you would like to INCREASE in your life. **Set an INTENTION that reflects how you want to feel about yourself at the end of the day.** Set an INTENTION to work towards YOUR dream. Set an INTENTION even when you cannot see how it can happen.

1. Look across the landscape of your life. What do you want to see there for yourself?

2. What are your standards?

3. Ask yourself, how do I want to feel about myself at the end of the day?

4. Did my choices and decisions match how I want to feel about myself?

Match you choices and decisions to how you want to feel about yourself.

*Match **YOUR** choices and behaviors towards **YOUR INTENTIONS** throughout the day, by taking a new **ACTION STEP.***

(I AM Choosing…)

Marianne, **YOU** *need to learn that you can handle life today just as it is.*

You *need to learn to stop WAITING for a later time to feel better.*

When you are not your REAL SELF you WAIT instead of just being and enjoying.

Be in today.

Don't be waiting for a better day. There is no more opportune time than today to feel better.

Be at peace with yourself.

(Managing Your Message)

5

OVERGIVING

OVERGIVING is a manipulative strategy to gain love and approval from other people, at great emotional cost to yourself. You believe how much you give to others is equated with being of value. If you do not EMOTIONALLY OWN your INHERENT VALUE, you can develop the distorted belief that the more you give, the more VALUE you will have. This thinking pattern is a trap. Why are you not valuable BEFORE you give? Why are YOU not enough? The OVERGIVING folks will often ask me, "How do I know if I am an OVERGIVER." There is a very simple answer. You are an OVERGIVER when you become ANGRY and ENRAGED and RESENTFUL towards the exact people you are OVERGIVING to in your life. Period.

When you are feeling "less than" you fear people will withdraw their love and approval. You struggle with setting boundaries by saying "NO" fearing others will be "angry with me and withdraw their love and approval." Your fear triggers the impulse to OVERGIVE. Your need for EXTERNAL validation and approval is often what motivated the OVERGIVING in the first place. Temporary EXTERNAL validation from others will not heal YOUR PRIMARY BELIEF OF BEING "LESS THAN." This BELIEF keeps you trapped in situations that are often draining the life blood out of you. You are emotionally exhausting yourself by trying to fix your INTERNAL world of emotional pain, by desperately seeking the EXTERNAL validation of others.

How you are using YOUR TIME provides great insight into how you emotionally feel about yourself. You are the steward of your precious TIME. It is YOUR twenty-four hours. How much of it are you giving away? When you are constantly OVERGIVING of your time and emotional energy, you may be seeking external validation and approval from others. I have found OVERGIVING people are some of the angriest and most hurting people walking around. You have a smile on the outside, yet inside you are emotionally exhausted and enraged. You have given-given-given far too much of your emotional energy to others, resulting in not having enough LIFE ENERGY for yourself. YOUR gas tank is less than empty, but you keep on OVERGIVING.

OVERGIVING is not a gift to others because it comes with a price tag you have "secretly" placed on the exchange. Your price tag is APPROVE OF ME – APPROVE OF ME - APPROVE OF ME – LOVE ME – LOVE ME – LOVE ME – MAKE ME FEEL WORTHY – MAKE ME FEEL WORTHY – MAKE ME FEEL WORTHY. God forbid if the person you are OVERGIVING to does not pay the price you expect, along with showing their undying gratitude for all the "sacrifices" you have made for them. Secretly, you know the "sacrifices" you have made have not been for them. **The "sacrifices" have been your unsuccessful attempt to PROVE YOUR INHERENT VALUE by desperately seeking the love and approval of others.** You are doing this by giving, giving, giving until YOU HURT. True giving is a gift with no expected return. You feel emotionally ENERGIZED when you truly give, not emotionally EXHAUSTED and ENRAGED. If you want to make a change in your behavior of OVERGIVING, you might consider taking an ACTION STEP of learning to say "NO."

When you say "NO" do not fall into the trap of feeling you are required to provide a good enough reason to justify your "NO." No reason or justification is needed. "NO" is all that is needed. Put a period at the end of your "NO." If you wish to give a reason, say it ONCE and then move on. When someone keeps asking you WHY NOT when you say "NO," they are not actually interested in YOUR reason. **They are continuing to push and shove you emotionally with the goal of triggering guilt, so you will change your mind.** A red flag should go up in your mind. They are only interested in the fact that they did not get what they wanted. They do not respect your "NO," clearly sending you the message in their behavior, that THEIR TIME is far more valuable than YOUR TIME. Your reason for saying "NO" is of little interest to them; their true motivation is that they did not get what they wanted from you.

Imagine if you asked a friend to drive you to an appointment and they responded by saying, "Sorry I can't help out this time." Would your response be, "WHAT, WHAT DO YOU MEAN NO, WHY NOT?" This response is rude and disrespectful of their time. When others attempt to push and shove you emotionally to change your mind, their behavior is demonstrating a clear lack of respect for you and your time. The good news is that you do not have to wait until others respect your time, as long as YOU RESPECT YOUR OWN TIME. **You control the time you keep for yourself, and how much time YOU CHOOSE to give away to others.**

Depending on your history, saying "NO" and putting yourself first may trigger a question in your mind; "Is saying NO allowed?" It is not only allowed, it is YOUR RESPONSIBILITY. Saying "NO" to some requests is a necessary tool for YOUR self care. If the idea of self care is emotionally difficult for you, considering the situation from another perspective may help. If you had a child would you wonder: Is it OK if I take care of the child's needs? Is it OK if I keep the child safe? Is it OK if I feed the child well? Is it OK if I comfort the child when they are scared? Is it OK to encourage them to find their voice and learn to speak for their needs? Is it OK to forgive and have compassion for the child's mistakes? If you do have children you may be thinking as a parent, what do you mean is it OK to take care of the BASIC NEEDS of my child! As a parent, I am RESPONSIBLE to care for their needs because they are valued and loved! When you accept you are RESPONSIBLE for every part of your child's well being, you can see the obvious. You are RESPONSIBLE FOR TAKING CARE OF EVERY PART OF YOUR WELL-BEING.

On the rare occasion when I feel pushed for not being able to meet a request and the person is attempting to manipulate me, I smile and give my reason by saying, "Because it is just not best for me at this time." No matter how many times they push, I give the same answer. I do not need to come up with a different answer to satisfy them, because I know their intention is to emotionally manipulate. This does not satisfy the other person, but it feels empowering not to give into their emotional manipulation. It is important to be willing to help out when you can, however you must balance how much time and energy you give away. Do not be emotionally manipulated into giving YOUR TIME away that you need for yourself. You will only be angry with yourself for doing so.

When someone in your life makes a request, a handy way of breaking the HABIT of quickly responding YES-YES-YES is to say, "I need twenty-four hours to think about it and I will get back to you." If they pressure you and say, "I need to know now," then the answer is simply "NO." When people continue to pressure you, call you selfish, or insist that you give your time away, the best thing to do is PAUSE. Give yourself time to feel if this is a request you want to help with, or is it best for YOU to say "NO." We all offer help at times when it may not be convenient. The difference in giving when it may not be convenient and OVERGIVING is that your main motivation is NOT seeking external approval. You want to make sure that OVERGIVING is not becoming your life's work. OVERGIVING until YOU HURT physically, emotionally and spiritually needs to be addressed as it leads to an increase in YOUR anger and resentment. I like to say, "If you say YES when you wanted to say NO, you forfeit your right to carry a resentment." The emotional exhaustion of OVERGIVING is destructive. Emotionally swimming in a pool of anger and resentment towards yourself and others for not saying "NO" is a painful way to spend the day.

You hurt yourself and others by denying your authentic self, and not respecting your own needs. This is a martyr mentality. You are not doing yourself or anyone any favors by not living authentically. You cannot take it out on others because you did not have the courage to validate your own needs by saying "NO." Being angry and raging on the inside with a smile on your face as you are OVERGIVING helps no one. Others will eventually be hurt some time in the future by being around an internally resentful person, who is spewing out displaced anger while smiling. No one is hurt when you make a decision to honor your authentic needs. **Although they may feel disappointed that they did not get what they wanted, their love for you does not change, unless you are involved with an OVERTAKER.**

OVERGIVING folks often find themselves in relationships with OVERTAKERS. OVERTAKERS are experts at emotional manipulation and know how to play the guilt card. If they emotionally manipulate you by threatening to withdraw their love to push for a YES, it is more important than ever to HONOR YOUR "NO." This manipulative exchange of energy is emotionally abusive behavior. When you make a choice to honor your needs first and someone attempts to emotionally manipulate you with guilt, limit the energy you give them, because they will NEVER be satisfied. You will run yourself into the ground physically and emotionally by OVERGIVING to an OVERTAKER. They will NEVER be happy and you will feel like you failed. In reality, you have disappointed yourself by denying your needs. When you deny your needs you are sending a very powerful negative message to yourself about your INHERENT VALUE. **Remember, you do not hurt anyone by being your true self and honoring your needs.**

You are also not responsible for finding a solution to the problem for the person or finding someone that will say YES. If you feel guilty for saying "NO," remember this dynamic is a learned HABIT. You may try and find a solution for the person to avoid feeling guilty. It is not because saying "NO" is the wrong decision to make for yourself. When practicing new behaviors old feelings will return, yet be determined to push past them with the INTENTION of improved self care. **You will begin to feel less and less guilt over time as you break the GUILT HABIT**

when you practice the self care tool of saying "NO." As you continue to practice this new ACTION STEP, you will look forward to the next time you can say "NO."

Yes, it is challenging to change the long held HABIT of OVERGIVING an immediate response of YES. However, once you face the newness and the fear of changing your behavior, you will experience how great it feels to take care of yourself first. Yes, I did say take care of yourself FIRST. You are not being selfish despite what others may say when they hear YOUR "NO," especially when they have learned to expect your YES-YES-YES. It is not selfish. You are responsible to care for yourself. Taking care of YOUR LIFE is your primary purpose.

Self care involves learning to say "NO" and also accepting other people's "NO." By honoring your life you are valuing the other person as well. Running after other people for their approval is an exhausting way to live. Use your energy instead to take care of yourself. Honoring YOUR life by definition is honoring the lives of all others. Devaluing YOUR life by definition devalues the lives of everyone you come in contact with in the world. **If you make SELF CARE a priority, you are less likely to fall prey to the need to OVERGIVE to be liked and loved.** When you are living authentically your need to seek external validation from others by OVERGIVING will be a thing of the past.

How are you using YOUR time?

1 2 3 4 5 6 7 8 9 10

Freely	OVERGIVING
Giving	Emotionally exhausted
Emotionally Energized	Smiling while enraged
	Resentful
	Angry with self for saying "YES" when you wanted to say "NO."

1.   On a scale from (1-10) what is your current number?

2.   When you say YES to a request when you wanted to say "NO" what is the number?

3.   Ask yourself what is your motivation for saying "YES" to a request?

4.   Are you seeking love and approval by OVERGIVING?

5.   Do you have an OVERTAKER in your life?

I was not born to relive my past. I was born to create today.

Everything ends in a perfect outcome despite how it begins, because I have learned.

I did not wake up to repeat the energy of yesterday.

I did not wake up to fear the energy of tomorrow.

I woke up today to create in the energy of NOW.
(Intention)

Move past your resentments *by working towards* **YOUR** *own***VICTORY**

(Overhelping)

6

OVERHELPING

Another relationship dynamic that backfires is OVERHELPING. OVERHELPING is pointing out the faults you find in another person, and MISTAKENLY BELIEVING they are going to thank you for your efforts. **OVERHELPING is offering YOUR OPINION regarding how you think others should be living their lives, when they have not asked for your opinion or feedback.** OVERHELPING sets you up for a pre-meditated resentment, when you have PRIOR expectations for others and they do not follow YOUR plan and agenda. You may attempt to justify OVERHELPING by saying, "I am only trying to be helpful." "I am only trying to help." Sounds good. However, a few important questions to ask yourself before you INSIST on offering your helpful suggestion are; has the person actually asked for your help? Have they sought out your opinion? Have they sought out your valuable counsel? Have they? If so, then by all means help out, share your important thought and then leave it to them to decide what to do with it. **Have NO emotional attachment as to whether or not they follow your suggestion.** When you become emotionally attached to the outcome, you can possibly cross the line into another form of destructive exchange of energy. This is the destructive energy of TRYING TO CONTROL ANOTHER PERSON'S BEHAVIOR - THOUGHTS - LIFE.

Trying to control other people does not come from a place of internal strength and security. It is driven from the energy of fear. Attempting to reduce your anxiety by trying to control the behavior of others only results in increasing YOUR fear. Don't make the mistake of believing you have the best answer for someone else's life. It is really an exhausting way for YOU to live. Your OVERHELPING in this way often alienates the exact people you are trying to help. The message you are sending them is, "I don't have faith in your ability to handle your life, to run your own race." **You are attempting to feel better about yourself by using other people.** This dynamic is NEVER a positive exchange of energy.

When someone is emotionally upset, it is not the best time to offer YOUR helpful tip. A respectful way to interact when you want to be helpful instead of controlling is to ask the person; "How can I be helpful?" Do not tell them what YOU feel they need. Try saying, "How can I be helpful? Do you want me to simply listen or are you looking for feedback?" If they ask you to LISTEN, giving your helpful TIP instead of simply listening is only going to make them feel worse. You are overriding their feelings and DEMONSTRATING by your actions that YOU know what is best for them. You will appear to be trying to control them after asking what THEY needed, and then disregarding what they have asked from you.

As a general rule this exchange of energy is not supportive and may demonstrate a self centeredness on your part. All you are doing is thinking about YOU and not about how to be helpful to them. It is important to be honest with yourself about YOUR INTENTION. Possibly you want to offer a quick solution, because you do not have the patience to listen or want to listen. You may want to solve the problem so YOU can be done, which is not often best for the other person. If being impatient is YOUR issue, practice giving the GIFT OF LISTENING without giving your opinion.

If you truly feel you have a valuable piece of information to share, wait twenty-four hours. Return to them and say something like, "I was thinking about your situation and I had an idea I thought might be helpful, is it something you are interested in hearing?" By checking it out BEFORE giving your thought, you continue demonstrating support in a respectful way. You are not just SHOUTING out your idea, ASSUMING the other person is interested in hearing your opinion. If your INTENTION is to be helpful to THEM, check it out first to see if they might be receptive.

This approach can make all the difference in how it will feel to be in a relationship with you. Simply ask, "How can I be helpful?" Then follow up!

OVERHELPING can result in becoming stuck in the emotional quicksand of feeling that no one is "appreciating" all that you are doing for them. This begins to build a fire of resentment. **You are not realizing that you resent others for not being more "appreciative" of your OVERHELPING, when YOU were the one who STARTED the negative exchange of energy.** By continuing to OVERHELP, you are throwing new logs of resentment on the fire. You feel "unappreciated" without realizing you are only burning yourself. THEY did not ask for your opinion in the first place. Stewing in your rage of feeling unappreciated, when YOU started the negative exchange by OVERHELPING is a destructive dynamic that is hurting you. **It is your OVERHELPING that leads to your resentment. It is NOT their lack of appreciation that is burning YOU and triggering your emotional distress.**

Another reason you may be inclined to OVERHELP is because you are afraid that if something were to happen to someone you love, you fear you would not be able to emotionally handle the situation (Worry Habit). Unfortunately, your attempt to OVERHELP and control results in increasing YOUR own fear. Your OVERHELPING is not motivated from a place of wanting to be helpful to the other person. It is being generated from an emotional place of feeling out of control yourself. **Displacing your fears onto someone else and wanting THEM to change so YOU can feel less anxious, is a devastating exchange of energy.** They will be angry with you for trying to control them. You will be angry that they are not willing to change, so you can feel less anxious. Now you are at a painful stalemate.

We want people in our lives to be cheering and supporting us on our OWN PATH. Who wants to be with someone who is continually yanking you off your path, trying to feel better about themselves at your expense? Other people in the world were not born to help you confirm your worth. You must validate it yourself. OVERGIVING and OVERHELPING behaviors will never result in peace for you. Never!

When you repeatedly practice breaking the HABIT of OVERGIVING your unsolicited opinion, you will experience many benefits. **The major benefit you will experience is that YOU are no longer triggering YOUR own anger, frustration and resentment when other people do not follow your unsolicited suggestions.** You will recognize over time that OVERHELPING was being triggered by YOUR fear. Unfortunately, the more you attempt to control other people to ease your fear the more anxious and fearful you will become, because YOU have no control over other people. **YOU have tied yourself to SELF GENERATED misery, when you stay trapped in the mental thinking pattern that others need to change and follow your unsolicited advice in order for you to be happy.** I can not emphasize enough the emotional benefits you will experience when you give up trying to run the world by OVERHELPING. You must experience how it feels yourself. The only way this can happen is to change the behavior of OVERHELPING. **You can set yourself free from this dynamic by practicing one simple yet challenging reality: STOP GIVING YOUR UNSOLICITED OPINION.** You need to experience the benefits yourself. You do have ABSOLUTE control over your choices and decisions. You will feel much less anxious and fearful when you simply focus only on your PATH, and stop offering YOUR unsolicited advice.

1. Keep track on a piece of paper how often in a twenty-four hour period of time you are giving your unsolicited opinions and suggestions.

2. Ask yourself, am I HELPING or am I OVERHELPING and being controlling? Basically, did anyone ask for your opinion before you offered it?

3. Objectively observe how other people are reacting to your OVERHELPING behavior.

4. If their reaction is negative, do you feel defensive, unappreciated and step into YOUR emotional quicksand of resentment?

5. Do you rehearse grievances over and over in your thinking and reach the conclusion that you were right?

6. Ask yourself, if I am offering supportive and loving energy, or am I forcing controlling energy/OVERHELPING?

*Only **LOVE** is needed.*

*Only **LOVE** will do.*

(Inherent Value)

*Developing a **peaceful friendship** with the realities of **change** and **uncertainty** is a life long process. Some days are better than others.* **<u>You can do it</u>**.

(Worry Habit)

7

WORRY HABIT

WORRY HABIT sets a powerful INTENTION for what you **DO NOT WANT** in the future. WORRY HABIT projects negative expectation of what you fear will happen in your life, and in the lives of those you love. WORRY HABIT is a strategy where people try and control what is not their place, or within their power to control. You are not controlling anything in the future by worrying today. You can also use the WORRY HABIT to deal with uncertainty, because you want a guaranteed result. Humans have a very difficult time with change, despite CHANGE being the natural order of the world. Very little in nature does not change, grow and evolve.

WORRY HABIT sets an expectation that something is going to go wrong in YOUR life. Your are unfortunately setting an INTENTION by finding fault with YOUR future. WORRY HABIT can ruin the present day because you are generating negative energy NOW, when you could be feeling happy, content, and enjoying your day. Projecting the constant energy of worry out into your life by THINKING, "What if this happens or what if that happens" is only destroying your enjoyment of the present moment.

WORRY HABIT is a dynamic you can learn and internalize from other people, without being aware of the long term consequences. Children observe their primary caretakers using the WORRY HABIT to manage their emotions and begin modeling what they are observing. Children can easily take on the WORRY HABIT as a way to feel they are controlling uncertainties and changes in their lives. They grow into adulthood using the WORRY HABIT strategy they have seen modeled around them. WORRY HABIT is a false belief, yet it can be learned and practiced as though it were a constructive way to manage YOUR emotions.

Your emotions follow your thinking patterns. You can be negatively impacting your day by creating a SCARY STORY in your thinking pattern that is not actually happening. The imaginary SCARY STORY is not real, but you are EMOTIONALLY reacting as if the SCARY STORY is actually happening. This dynamic impacts your feelings and mood. You can ruin your entire day by feeling afraid of the SCARY STORY you have been telling yourself, when all is actually going well in the present moment. **The imaginary SCARY STORY you are REHEARSING and REPLAYING in your head about the future, is what is triggering your anxious emotional reaction**. You may be feeling emotional pain and want it to stop. You are NOT realizing that YOU are the one generating the emotional distress, by creating and dwelling on your imaginary SCARY STORIES. You only increase your anxiety by giving voice to the SCARY STORY repeating it to other people.

When you create a SCARY STORY in your imagination about what may happen in the future, these thinking patterns automatically impact your mood and emotions. **When your thinking pattern is focused on telling itself a SCARY STORY, your emotional world will respond and reflect the SCARY STORY.** If you are creating a story in your thinking that is filled with joy, peace and expectation of good outcomes, then your emotions will reflect these thoughts. If however, you are creating a SCARY STORY about what MIGHT happen in the FUTURE or are reliving painful memories from the past, then your emotions and mood will reflect this process.

I will ask people when they are upset, what they have been thinking about. They typically respond by saying, "I have no idea what I am thinking about, I am just really upset and feel bad." You believe your painful emotions are coming for an external source, and look to change external events to reduce your uncomfortable feelings, often without success. When you take a moment and step back, pause, breathe, and focus on what you are actually imagining, you begin to see a connection between your thinking patterns and how you are feeling. **By challenging your distorted thinking patterns and imaginary SCARY STORIES, you can change your mood and how you feel.**

Imagine you are sitting at the beach on vacation and looking out at the beautiful ocean. Your mind is racing with the argument you had last night with a friend. You are angrily THINKING about all

53

the things you forgot to say, and plan to say next time you see them. You are sitting in a moment of tranquility at the ocean, but your THINKING PATTERN is ruminating on an angry argument that is being created by YOU and only taking place in your head (Worry Habit). Your mood is angry and upset over something that is not actually happening NOW, or probably will never happen in the future. You are missing out on enjoying the tranquil experience of the calm ocean.

Have you ever noticed that when you are having an imaginary argument in your head with someone, YOU always have the best things to say, and THEY always have the stupid things to say? You feel you are winning the argument and have the moral high ground, when you are engaging in an imaginary argument. You feel you are in complete control of the fantasy and what is happening. This gives you a sense of being RIGHT and winning. But are you really winning? **If you cannot enjoy this peaceful moment at the ocean without raising your blood pressure, pulse and anger level due to your IMAGINARY argument, have you actually won?** What exactly did you win? No, you have lost. You have missed out on enjoying your day at the ocean, while your friend is probably sitting at the lake enjoying the day without a thought of you. No external event is causing PRESENT MOMENT distress. It is the scary/angry story you are creating and dwelling on in your imagination that is triggering YOUR emotional pain. Rehearsing your resentments or enjoying the ocean is your choice. **CHOOSE WISELY.**

Internalizing the WORRY HABIT energy of others leaves YOU with unhappiness and suffering that does not belong to you. Sometimes others want you to take on their negative energy, and will be harping until you are in the same mood. Misery loves company as they say, and this can be true for you if you are not careful. Well meaning people can dump the energy of their fears on to you by saying; "What would you do if that happens?" "What will you do if that does not happen?" **It is life-saving to work towards not internalizing the emotional energy and fears of other people.** I encourage you to keep it within the day and focus on what is happening at that time IN YOUR LIFE. It is not your responsibility to carry the fears and anxieties of others. Nor is it your responsibly to resolve these fears for others, because it is not possible. You can support people, but you cannot resolve their internal emotional issues. This is their work to do. They must do it for themselves and emotionally own the reward by taking action and making changes in their own lives.

One way to begin to challenge and change your WORRY HABIT is replacing "what if" SCARY STORIES with a new PERSONAL MANTRA. Your new mantra might sound like, "Well, if or when it does happen, I will take care of it at that time." By adjusting your thought patterns in the present moment, you are not putting your head in the sand and saying nothing bad or painful will ever happen. What you are doing is setting the INTENTION today, that when something challenging happens in the future, you are more than capable of taking care of it AT THAT TIME.

A new thought mantra replaces the WORRY HABIT thought pattern and supports a more productive way to handle problems. Allowing yourself the opportunity to focus on the new thought helps to change your emotional reaction from worry/anxiety, to feeling empowered. By setting an INTENTION that YOU will resolve problems when they happen, develops confidence today that you will be able to take appropriate action at that time. **NOW, you can enjoy the moment without being impacted by the emotional cloud of worry/fear/anxiety that YOU created in your imagination.** Practice challenging the negative thinking patterns of today's WORRY HABIT.

When you experience painful emotions you usually focus on the feelings, because that is the painful energy you are experiencing. You may not take the time to look at what has been your thinking focus. Sometimes, your thoughts can be distorted. Reality testing these distortions is another self care tool that will positively impact your mood directly. Building confidence in your ability to manage difficult issues is an important element of EMOTIONAL MATURITY. **You may have to repeat YOUR new personal mantra over and over again when the thoughts of worry flood back in, because they will.** This process will becomes easier and more natural the more you practice.

When you become aware of the WORRY HABIT continue to practice a mantra like, "When or if it happens I will take care of it at that time." You are not pretending that something potentially can't go wrong in the future. You are reinforcing YOUR power by repeating the mantra, "I will take care of it." **You are setting a POWERFUL INTENTION for the future; if something happens I have confidence in myself to be able to resolve the issue.** You realize worrying beforehand becomes pointless and unnecessary. **Worrying NOW about something that may or may not happen in the future, will NOT result in your feeling more in control today.** The WORRY HABIT evokes an out of control feeling and keeps it burning. You negate the power to create today. Impacting YOUR future by the WORRY HABIT only sets an INTENTION for what YOU DO NOT WANT. Do you want to create in your life what you are currently focusing on?

I have used this strategy in my own life dealing with heart arrhythmia problems. I was born with a heart arrhythmia. Without warning my heart would suddenly start beating in an abnormal rhythm.

As I grew older the episodes of the arrhythmia became more frequent. I was fine one moment and literally, in the next second, my heart would start to race and beat out of rhythm. There was no predicting when or where it might start, or when it would stop and return to a normal heart rhythm (talk about uncertainty). Throughout my life I would often have WORRY HABIT thoughts of "WHAT IF" I was driving on the highway, at work, or home alone in a snow storm and my heart went out of rhythm. Could I get help? How would I get help? The arrhythmia would start and stop within a matter of one or two minutes, and other times my heart would beat out of rhythm for many hours. When I turned forty I started to have a different type of arrhythmia. Now I was dealing with two different heart arrhythmias that were becoming more frequent. Wondering where I would be if my heart went out of rhythm continued to increase the scary "what if" stories in my head. This triggered an increase in my WORRY HABIT and anxiety.

I continually practiced challenging my "WHAT IF" thinking patterns that were triggering my fear. I CONTINUALLY WORKED to change my thinking pattern from "what if" to "when and if it happens I will deal with it at that time. NOW it is not happening, so I can be at peace." When my fears raced in, repeating that I will deal with it when it happens helped me to break my pattern of using the WORRY HABIT, as a way to try and control what was uncontrollable. **WORRY HABIT had not made me feel more in control; all it was doing was increasing my anxiety.** The episodes of irregular heart rhythms were increasing in frequency, and trips to the Emergency Room were common. I was working at the time doing Psychiatric and Addiction Evaluations in the Emergency Department, when suddenly I would go from being a staff member to being admitted as a patient.

I decided to have a surgical procedure to correct the problem. On the morning of my surgery I remember very specifically the doctor saying to me, "Are you ready to say goodbye to an old friend?" I thought this was a very interesting way to see the situation, as this medical issue had been with me my entire life. I thought about what the doctor said that day. I realized by the time I was having this procedure in my early forties, I was more at peace with how to live with the reality of uncertainties in my life. My issue of wanting to control EXTERNAL things as a way to deal with my anxiety/fear around change and uncertainty had lessened, due to many years of discipline on the issue. I had trained myself not to give in to the anxiety of "what if" when it started in my thinking. Instead, I repeatedly focused on the thought, "If something happens I will deal with it at that time." I no longer needed my irregular heart beat to teach me how to handle the uncertainty of life. I had learned what I needed to learn from this challenge, and was indeed ready to say goodbye to this old friend.

A personal test on the issue of letting go of the WORRY HABIT came shortly after my heart procedure. A year prior to needing the surgery I had planned a trip to Greece. The reality of this surgical procedure is that it may not work, and you have to go back to the operation table for a second time. There is no way to predict if the surgery is successful until you wait one day, one week, one month, six months to see if the arrhythmia returns. The doctor could not tell if the surgery had been successful, until time passed to prove I would no longer have the arrhythmia.

My trip to Greece was already planned and fell six weeks after my surgery. My doctor said I was medically fine to go but added, "If the procedure did not work, the worst that can happen is you will have the same problem, nothing new." My IMMEDIATE thoughts were, "What if I am on an airplane going to Greece and my heart goes out of beat while I am over the ocean?" "Will I be able to get help?" "It is too risky to go, I have to cancel my trip." **Why is it that the negative/fearful thoughts seem to pop in first!** I DECIDED my "what if" thinking pattern was not going to ruin what I had been looking forward to all year. I did not let my WORRY HABIT get the best of me. I kept repeating my mantra daily and all the way to the plane and beyond.

Many times while climbing the mountains in Greece random THOUGHTS popped up reminding me that hope for medical attention was hours away. I remember thinking on more than one occasion, "Not sure this was the best idea." A moment of comedy came one day when I was walking on a hot afternoon up the side of a mountain. I noticed many elderly people smoking while climbing up the same mountain. I thought, "Wow if they have a heart attack how will they get help?" How easily I can project my fears onto other people, and trigger my own anxiety. I continued to calm my fears with my mantra, "I will take care of it when and if it happens." I went to Greece and had a wonderful time. I have been stable for over eleven years.

The WORRY HABIT provides a temporary false sense of control. To break the WORRY HABIT you need to train yourself to develop confidence by successfully overcoming challenges at the TIME THEY HAPPEN, and NOT BEFORE. **You develop YOUR confidence by giving up the WORRY HABIT and replacing it with YOUR new MANTRA and TAKING ACTION.** Have a CORRECTIVE EXPERIENCE by taking a risk to approach the problem in a different way. Do not avoid the issue and hope it will disappear.

As you continue to practice, you will experience your personal mantra coming to mind far more easily. Any WORRY HABIT THOUGHTS that creep in will slink away as you identify the "what if" thoughts, bid them farewell, and replace them with YOUR new MANTRA. When you repeatedly demonstrate you are able to resolve challenges at the time they happen, the periods between problems can be lived emotionally in peace, joy and calm. Yes, I did say calm. You can make it happen. Don't miss a calm moment by ruminating about an imaginary SCARY STORY in your thoughts. It is your BELIEF that is creating the increased emotional fear. Saying, "Yes, I can handle painful emotional issues when they happen" greatly reduces fearful energy now, because you are setting a POWERFUL INTENTION of accomplishment in the future. You are more than capable of handling any situation. **Refocusing your thoughts from fear to VICTORY changes your energy in the present moment**.

You are gifted with the biological ability for fight or flight. This innate skill helps to keep you safe and alive. However, you can overuse this ability and wear yourself down. **You can be living in a fight or flight energy level twenty-four hours a day in your thought pattern, always preparing for what you fear MIGHT happen.** Your thinking pattern may be keeping you in a fight or flight level of fearful energy, when in reality everything is really going well in your present moment/day.

What kind of thinking pattern are you living in today? I encourage people when they are feeling emotional distress, anxiety, or anger to look at the present moment, take a couple of breaths and ask themselves, "Is anything actually going wrong at this moment? Is there a dog actually chasing me, or is my WORRY HABIT of creating an imaginary SCARY STORY working overtime?" When you feel yourself PHYSICALLY tense and stressed, notice what you are thinking about. Again, is the dog actually chasing you? Is this a problem or crisis that is actually happening in the present moment that warrants the adrenaline rush of fight or flight? Are you creating a fearful story in your head today about something that might happen in the future? **Are you becoming emotionally upset because of the created SCARY STORY?** How is your SCARY STORY impacting you physically?

Your "what if" thinking patterns can lead to a significant increase in emotional stress and anxiety. **You are not only missing out on experiencing peace in the moment, but your body and emotions are reacting as though the "what if" scenario is actually happening.** Ask yourself, is there a dog actually chasing me in the present moment? If he is, then by all means take off running and resolve the IMMEDIATE problem or crisis. If not, is it worth having your day ruined by an imaginary SCARY STORY you are creating? Do you want to ride this emotionally exhausting thought loop in your head all day?

Even when you work hard to make improvements in you life, peaceful times may feel unfamiliar, uncomfortable and even anxiety provoking. The WORRY HABIT of waiting for the next bad thing to happen, impacts your enjoyment of the present moment. Even when everything is actually going well, your WORRY HABIT may be sapping your enjoyable energy. No dog is actually chasing you. The reality is that you could be enjoying your day fully.

On a scale from 0-10 how are you using your energy?

10 - Full day of enjoyable energy
5 - Enjoyable energy + 5 worry habit energy
2 - Enjoyable energy + 8 worry habit energy
0 - Enjoyable energy +10 worry habit energy

The thoughts you are focusing on in your thinking pattern you experience as EMOTIONALLY true. If you struggle with having confidence in your ability to manage your life, you may cultivate the WORRY HABIT attempting to gain a sense of control. You hope that by worrying enough about everything, nothing bad will happen. This is magical thinking and will let you down. The reality of human life is that events will happen that are difficult and emotionally painful. **The goal is to develop enough confidence within yourself to believe; I know that if or when something happens I will be able to take care of the problem at that time.**

Begin setting an INTENTION to enjoy a few peaceful moments each day. Take note of what is going well in the moment, add some present moment gratitude and feel yourself relax. Learning over time to trust your INTERNAL WISDOM and believing it will guide you to YOUR best answer is worth the effort. Remember, just because you are thinking something does not make it true. The importance of learning to identify, challenge, and move past the negative first thought cannot be overstated (Thought Cascade). Being ever vigilant regarding what you allow yourself to focus on is worth the effort. Developing a peaceful friendship with the realities of change and uncertainty is a life long process. Some days are better than others. You can do it.

Relax Gently   Live Gently

1.   Are you watering your weeds (Negative Thoughts) or are you watering your flowers (Intentions)?

2.   Identify two WORRY HABIT thought patterns?

3.   Do they belong to you, or did you learn them from someone else?

4.   What is YOUR new PERSONAL MANTRA?

5.   What is the impact of WORRY HABIT on your physical health?

Fear costs everything.
Love is Free.

Fear evaporates energy for life.
Love is the life blood of energy for life.

Shame negates all energy for life.
Love negates shame for self and others.

Blame and put downs are shame.
Love only uplifts and inspires.

It costs you tremendous energy not to love.

It costs you nothing in energy to
LOVE.

(Emotional Manipulation is Fear Energy)

shame *is based on*

<u>**NOTHING**</u>

(Inherent Value)

8

FAIRNESS PATROL

Being out on FAIRNESS PATROL is wasting YOUR precious time ACTIVELY noticing what other people (including complete strangers) are doing wrong, from a mindset of fault finding. You then spend an inordinate amount of time having IMAGINARY CONVERSATIONS with yourself, about what you think others should or should not be doing according to your rules of life. Spending time in your head telling complete strangers what you think they should or should not do is an interesting hobby, and a destructive waste of your time. **FAIRNESS PATROL is a self imposed burden.**

You may be out on FAIRNESS PATROL for many reasons and not actually be aware of the time you are wasting. A FAIRNESS PATROL mindset can be motivated by emotional states such as:

1. Boredom with yourself and life.
2. Hobby/habit. Too much free time.
3. Anger – looking for a reason to justify anger.
4. Temporarily feeling "better than" others.

5. Feeling "less than" about yourself.
6. Wanting to feel in control when you are not.

Cultivating the HABIT of being out on FAIRNESS PATROL comes from a place of fear and needing to feel in control, by shifting the focus from yourself to others. This can temporarily distract you from focusing on changes YOU need to be making in your own life. You have somehow convinced yourself that the UNIVERSE needs your help directing the lives of other humans on the planet. You may feel you have taken on a great burden in helping the UNIVERSE run more smoothly. You feel very justified in handing down your judgments of others, without realizing the negative emotional impact on yourself.

JUDGING others will ALWAYS leave you with negative energy, no matter how strongly you feel other people were deserving of your judgments. YOU have only generated an increase in YOUR anger/agitation/frustration all the while believing it was the OTHER PERSON WHO triggered your negative/painful feelings. You do not realize that this increase in negative/painful feelings is coming from YOUR very busy day out on FAIRNESS PATROL. Take the time to observe how you feel after a busy day on FAIRNESS PATROL. You will be able to observe the negative impact on your mood and how much time and energy you are wasting, which may motivate you to address YOUR behavior.

The first step to motivating change is to become aware of how being out on FAIRNESS PATROL is negatively impacting YOUR energy and mood. While on FAIRNESS PATROL visualize each of your JUDGEMENTS as a ball of negative energy you are collecting in a backpack and carrying around the entire day. What size balls of negative energy/judgements are you collecting? Are you amassing golf balls-baseballs-footballs-basketballs-bowling balls or cannon balls of negative energy? Do you need to strap on another backpack when you run out of room in the first one? Are you even out of the house in the morning before your first backpack is full? How is your mood and energy level? Increased awareness allows for choices. **Now you have the POWER to continue with the same HABITUAL behaviors on FAIRNESS PATROL or CHOOSE to make a change.**

This may sting your ego a little, but the stranger/person YOU are judging while out on FAIRNESS PATROL do not even notice you. They do not care that you exist. They have no interest in knowing your opinion regarding what YOU believe they were doing WRONG, or what YOU believe they should be doing differently. To be motivated to change YOUR behavior, it is important to read those last three sentences again. Accept this reality. They do not know YOU exist. YOU are only wasting YOUR time. Have you ever stopped to wonder what faults other people out on FAIRNESS PATROL are observing in YOU? That reality may sting a little as well. You are only hurting YOURSELF with self generated pain. You may mistakenly think it is EXTERNAL people, places and situations that are CAUSING you pain. **When you stop long enough to observe your behavior, you realize that YOU are GENERATING and collecting the unnecessary misery.** You could have easily left the negative energy in the past by recognizing your FAIRNESS PATROL behavior. The anger and agitation YOU generate in your thinking pattern while on FAIRNESS PATROL is a self inflicted wound.

Another option to relieve yourself of the self-imposed burden of feeling you are responsible for running the world on FAIRNESS PATROL is to consider the following: Unless you are directly notified at the beginning of the day that the UNIVERSE needs you to intervene/interfere in the lives of others, you can consider yourself off the hook and take the day off. If the Universe is not directly in contact with you to start your day, you can feel relieved of this self imposed burden. While you take this time off from keeping watch, you have the day to keep the focus on YOU and what YOU are creating in your day. Your day will be remarkably simpler if you keep your focus on the following:

YOUR attitude.
YOUR behavior.
YOUR choices.
How YOU treat others.
How YOU treat yourself.

In my twenties one of my old HABITS was being out on FAIRNESS PATROL on a daily basis. I looked to judge and find fault with people who were not following MY RULES. I often seemed to be looking for opportunities to be angry. I could stuff several backpacks a day with my negative

65

balls of energy. Until I knew better, I felt very justified in my JUDGEMENTS when I perceived that others were breaking MY rules. One of my old behaviors was counting how many items someone had in the quick check out line. When the sign read "ten items or less," and the person ahead of me had twelve items, I could feel my judgmental energy rising to the surface. This judgmental energy would mix with the energy of my self-righteous anger. Just when I was feeling "angry superiority" the person would suddenly reach over and pick up a pack of gum and a candy bar. Well, now they had fourteen items, the sign says ten items and I have eight items. I followed MY RULES, they did not.

Of course I would never say anything to the person, but inside I was fuming. I could keep this fuming energy going all the way out to my car. On a bad day, I ruminated on the negative energy all the way home. The person in front of me with the fourteen items went along their way and probably enjoyed their day. All I had done was create a miserable mood due to MY need to make sure everyone else in the world was following MY RULES. You may say, "They should follow the rules." Maybe so, but is it worth all the negative misery you are generating in your thinking. It is your thinking pattern that is triggering your angry mood. **It is NOT the person's behavior, it is how you are interpreting and reacting to the situation that is causing you distress (Emotional Maturity).**

The good news is that you do not have to wait until everyone in the world has "ten items or less" to feel peaceful. You can CHOOSE to feel peaceful despite what anyone else is doing. It was my need to judge others that was triggering my distress, NOT that they had fourteen items when the sign said ten. I realized that my need to judge only spoke about me and how I was feeling about myself at that time in my life. I was looking for some reason to be angry EXTERNALLY, so I could avoid addressing the issues that I needed to be working on myself. **Do not let the outside world control how you feel.** Control how you feel by letting go of situations that are really none of your business. I have learned my life is so much more peaceful when I just keep on MY PATH and stop interfering in the world by being out on FAIRNESS PATROL. Today, if I notice myself out of HABIT counting items while standing in line, I turn my focus around. **I remind myself that other people are not responsible for how I feel or how I react in ANY situation**. INSTEAD, I focus on gratitude in the present moment that I recognized this old behavior. I am grateful that I no longer waste my precious time running the world out on FAIRNESS PATROL.

You may be unsure if you engage in FAIRNESS PATROL behaviors. Driving on the roads allows you a perfect view to observe your behavior and identify any tendency towards being on

FAIRNESS PATROL. I believe the term you may have heard is ROAD RAGE. Your ROAD RAGE, not their driving. Does it sound at all familiar? Awareness of behavior empowers you to make a CHOICE and DECISION to move towards change.

If you are unsure if you have a tendency towards being out on FAIRNESS PATROL try the following experiment:

1. Observe and write down how often in one day you notice and comment to yourself in YOUR THINKING about others not performing in the world according to your standards/rules. What is the number?

2. Keep track of the number of times in a twenty-four hour period you have focused on the faults in STRANGERS. What is the number?

3. What is your mood like at the end of the day?

4. How many balls of negative energy/judgements were in YOUR backpack?

5. Did you have any time today to achieve and accomplish YOUR GOALS?

It is energizing to work on **CHANGING** and **GROWING** aspects of yourself, rather than being exhausted by expending so much energy trying to HIDE behind **YOUR** facade.

(Inherent Value)

Release me from **MY** *chain of unforgiving energy.*

Holding onto **MY** *own chain of unforgiving energy holds* **ME** *underwater.*

*Simply let go of YOUR chain and easily float to the surface. Take a big breath of **forgiveness**.*

You *were suffocating yourself all along by holding* **YOUR** *chain tight, and NEEDING to be* **RIGHT**.

(Overhelping)

9

Managing YOUR Message

Managing YOUR Message is when you PERFORM in the world with the goal of trying to manipulate others into having a favorable opinion of you. **You work hard to create a positive message about yourself in the mind of others, while secretly suffering in a place of feeling "less than."** You put aside your true feelings, thoughts, and desires. You create a character and perform for the world. **You PRETEND to be how you want others to see you.** What you are presenting is a facade. People will work for years trying to fix themselves, while expending so much life energy being a false person, or acting out a persona for others. All along they fear their behavior will be exposed as a facade. They remain very afraid that the truth will be exposed, so work hard to manage the message. **The NEGATIVE MESSAGE you are continually sending to yourself while you are acting the façade is the ultimate ENERGY of SELF REJECTION.**

You can begin to develop this strategy at a young age. For example, the child will say the game being played is "silly and stupid." They say, "I didn't want to play anyway" as a way to avoid the risk of wanting to be included, and then not being chosen for the team. The child attempts to give off the air of indifference of not wanting to be included, to avoid feeling fear of possibly being excluded. It is less emotionally painful to say, I did not want something, than take the risk of being vulnerable and feel the humiliation of not being included.

You create a façade for emotional protection. You work to persuade others to like/love you to avoid feeling rejection. If the façade gets rejected, then "I" really did not get rejected. The downside of this exchange of energy is that if others like and care for you, YOU KNOW they love and care for the façade, not the real you. Although you can MANAGE YOUR MESSAGE and create an enviable façade, anyone who is living behind this false front knows that this is an "excruciatingly" emotionally painful way to live. Possibly you have reached a point that YOU really do not know who you actually are today. The years of living the façade have made it difficult to connect to the real you. This can be emotionally terrifying. To protect yourself, you further add to the persona by feigning indifference to your own needs.

You can use the same strategy of MANAGING YOUR MESSAGE to protect yourself from feeling vulnerable. To avoid feeling vulnerable you learned to MANAGE YOUR MESSAGE in many ways. You MANAGE YOUR MESSAGE by pretending to yourself and others that you never feel: sad-angry-disappointed-lonely-embarrassed-left out. You MANAGE YOUR MESSAGE to avoid acknowledging your fear of not fitting in or being included. You pretend to yourself and others that being part of the group/team is not important to you. You pretend that you can't be hurt or bothered by anything or anyone. **It is less emotionally painful to PRETEND you didn't really want something, than to take the emotional risk of wanting it, and not having it work out.** The façade helps you avoid acknowledging the pain of feeling left out, pretending you cannot be hurt or disappointed. You work hard to give the impression that you are above it all, while internally you feel emotionally buried by it all.

Risking vulnerability is not what is causing the pain. SELF REJECTION is causing the emotional pain. The energy of SELF REJECTION (façade) is emotional quicksand. The more you struggle pretending to be the façade, the faster you sink into more self created emotional suffering. **It hurts to be rejected by others in your life, however to be REJECTING YOURSELF by being the facade each day is so much more devastating.** The message you are basically sending yourself is that the truth of who you are must be hidden, which triggers the energy of SHAME. SHAME is a state of being. **You can frantically look for EXTERNAL ways to numb the SHAME, without realizing that YOU are triggering the feelings of shame by YOUR self rejection.** You are not realizing that it is being trigged by the dynamic of MANAGING YOUR MESSAGE and rejecting yourself and your own needs.

MANAGING YOUR MESSAGE smothers any opportunity for emotional growth and learning. If you succeed as the façade, you really do not feel that you own the victory. Because that little voice in the back of your head continues whispering, that you might someday be found out and accused of being a fraud. Even if others never find out the truth, YOU know, and that is what is causing the emotional pain. MANAGING YOUR MESSAGE denies your reality. You are denying your INHERENT VALUE which goes against why YOU were SPECIFICALLY born. It negates what you have to offer. It nullifies what the rest of the world needs you to authentically contribute.

How can you begin to work towards making a change, when you are not ready to take an ACTION STEP into your life? You can begin by simply observing how you are MANAGING YOUR MESSAGE now. Use your imagination to create how you may in the future handle a similar situation more authentically. You are in complete control. Imagine handling the situation from the perspective of living from your INHERENT VALUE. Replay the scenario over and over in your imagination. Generate feelings of confidence in your ability to take the ACTION STEP when you are ready. You only need to keep imagining it, and when you are ready the true you will naturally flow out.

Your responsibility is to work to accept yourself at the present moment to the best of your ability. Part of this process is identifying areas of your personality that you want to grow and develop. It is rewarding to work on CHANGING and GROWING aspects of yourself, rather than being exhausted by expending so much energy in trying to HIDE behind your facade. You GAIN when you change and grow, and remain stagnant when you hide. You will need to expend energy either way. What do you want to use your emotional energy for; MANAGING YOUR MESSAGE (hiding) or CHANGING and GROWING?

When YOU risk taking an ACTION STEP you will feel YOUR power and realize that HIDING behind your facade is what is CAUSING the fear. **It is HIDING that is triggering the feeling of shame, because YOU are rejecting YOURSELF.** Life offers many people that will accept us and those that will reject us. You are more than capable of handling this dynamic. Self acceptance or self rejection by MANAGING YOUR MESSAGE is the only energy YOU ultimately control, and is the only energy that will impact what YOU create in YOUR life. It is not what others think of you that is the issue, but what you BELIEVE about yourself. Why spend so much time being

preoccupied with what others think because they are not creating your life. **YOU are the CREATOR.**

1.   When did you begin to MANAGE YOUR MESSAGE?

2.   Do you continue to MANAGE YOUR MESSAGE to protect yourself from being hurt?

3.   How can you find the courage to shed the false persona and take the risk to allow people to see the real you?

4.   What is YOUR first ACTION STEP towards a more authentic life?

Limitation and emotional bondage is living on someone else's path. Break out to emotional **FREEDOM** *and travel with ease on YOUR* ***OWN PATH.***

(My Path)

I open and expand my heart to full acceptance of all that I am - all that I have done, with the relief of knowing I did the best with what I knew.

NOW *is another moment.*

*It will be lived with **JOY** and a **SMILE**.*

(Emotional Maturity)

10

CORRECTIVE EXPERIENCE

Emotionally experience your INHERENT VALUE by having what I like to call a "CORRECTIVE EXPERIENCE" in the present moment. **The goal of a CORRECTIVE EXPERIENCE is to learn and grow NOW, by taking a new ACTION STEP in OPPOSITION to your past HABITUAL behaviors.** Developing the courage to take an ACTION STEP in opposition to your old behavioral HABITS is the beginning of CHANGE.

Changing your actions and behaviors towards yourself immediately reconnects you with the energy of your INTERNAL WISDOM. Reconnecting with your INTERNAL WISDOM is the first part of the process. The challenge is when you identify the guidance of your INTERNAL WISDOM will YOU have the courage to follow? When your INTERNAL WISDOM is leading you away from what allows you to feel emotionally safe, you may avoid listening out of fear of CHANGE and UNCERTAINTY. Even when you are feeling emotionally stagnant and desperately want so many things in your life to be different, YOUR fear is a barrier to change. Also, it can feel emotionally paralyzing to make a change when you feel trapped, or others are displacing THEIR ENERGY of FEAR onto you.

One BELIEF that stunts motivation for a CORRECTIVE EXPERIENCE is the following; Because of my PAST I am trapped and cannot create a new future. Why this thinking pattern is such a trap is because YOUR PAST will never be different – it is over – done – not to be relived. If you feel that you cannot have what you would like in YOUR PRESENT DAY because of your PAST, you are basically setting an INTENTION that YOUR life will never be what YOU want, so why bother trying. This BELIEF keeps you apathetic and you struggle to motivate yourself to work on having a CORRECTIVE EXPERIENCE to change.

YOUR thinking pattern of "I am trapped" suggests something or someone OUTSIDE of yourself is in charge, and is keeping you from making a change. This thinking pattern allows you to forgo responsibility for addressing your fear of CHANGE and UNCERTAINTY. You want to have a guarantee of success before you are willing to take the risk and start. The energy this thinking pattern creates is that no change is possible because "I'm trapped." No, you are not trapped. Imagine you are in a traffic jam and a car is two inches in front of you and two inches behind you. You have not moved one inch for six hours due to the traffic jam. This is what it means to be trapped, with no power to make a change in your situation.

You are NOT trapped! It is a CHOICE you are making, not something that is happening to you. You are either deciding to make a change OR you are deciding not to make a change and remain standing still. Don't emotionally take on the "poor me" role of saying, "I'm trapped there is nothing I can do." Feeling trapped is often a by-product of YOUR fear of CHANGE and not wanting to fail or be embarrassed.

Having a CORRECTIVE EXPERIENCE in the present moment is one of the most effective strategies to challenge YOUR belief pattern of being trapped by your past. CORRECTIVE EXPERIENCES involve moving out of your comfort zone and taking a new ACTION STEP. Taking a new ACTION STEP is the opposite of sitting back with fingers crossed hoping change will just happen, with no effort or risk on your part. Taking an ACTION STEP eliminates your behavior of blaming others that your life is not changing for the better. Setting YOUR INTENTION needs to be followed by taking an ACTION STEP. REPEATING your ACTION STEP helps to build confidence to keep moving towards what you want to be creating in YOUR life. Taking an ACTION STEP allows you to experience life differently, and feel the emotional benefit of taking the risk to make a change and expand your life.

Despite your belief in being "less than," taking an ACTION STEP DEMONSTRATES A BOLD STATEMENT OF YOUR INHERENT VALUE. Listening to your INTERNAL WISDOM and trusting it is not a one time event. Connection to your INTERNAL WISDOM needs continual attention. REPEATEDLY taking small ACTION STEPS on your behalf releases healing energy. Experience what it feels like to value your needs and desires. Experience what it is like to take care of yourself. When you experience your INTERNAL WISDOM working on your behalf, it becomes very hard to return to the prior stagnation.

You will experience emotional freedom by being willing to take the risk of creating something new, EVEN WHEN YOU MAKE A MISTAKE. **Mistakes are a part of the human experience.** Do not call yourself names when you make a mistake. Identify what can be different and what new options are available. Return to the challenge with the goal of correcting the mistake and working out the issue. COURSE CORRECT by not personalizing the mistake, dealing with the issue, and making another decision. As long as there has been learning you can move past the mistake by taking the gift of what you have learned into the future. I often hear people say, "Well I have a second chance to make things better." Telling yourself you have a second chance keeps bringing the energy of the past disappointment with you. Remember, the present moment is always a FIRST OPPORTUNITY for a new adventure.

One of the most helpful ways I have found to work towards emotional resolution and not keep recreating the past is to seek out the learning in the present moment. You may have to look long and hard, but the gift of learning and having a CORRECTIVE EXPERIENCE is always an option. First, ask yourself, "What is my learning" and bring that wisdom forward into your life. Second, use what you have learned to be of help to someone else in the future. When I seek the learning for myself, I eventually realize that I have overcome the difficulty and brought a benefit forward into my life. When I am then able to use the learning to help someone else, it give purpose and meaning to the event.

I used this approach when my father suddenly passed away. For many years I had practiced the self care skill that when something painful happened and triggered anxiety/fear, I would remind myself as **quickly as possible** that no matter the situation, I would learn from the experience. This gave me something other than the pain to focus on. Shortly after seeing my father in the hospital the day he died, an intense but clear thought popped into my head, "There is going to be great learning for you in this." It was not that it made the grief easier, but it helped me to keep looking for the learning as I coached myself through the grief process.

I had feared the UNCERTAINTY of potential loss my entire life. My historical pattern many years prior had been to close down emotionally and avoid dealing with the pain of actual loss or fear of loss. I can honestly say that what I learned through the process of grieving my father's loss were lessons I could have only learned with his passing. It was not that I would have wanted him to go so soon, but he did pass. I could have stayed stuck in the grief by avoiding it or seek out the lessons in the experience. I learned many things about myself during this time, but the most important lesson I learned was that I can emotionally survive and grow through great loss. I am no longer emotionally paralyzed by the fear of possible loss. I no longer try to control life to avoid potential loss. This realization and learning developed over many years. It was not easy or without challenging times, but knowing I was open to learning, helped me to find the gift in the pain.

The gift I now EMOTIONALLY OWN is that no matter the losses I will face in the future, I will learn and grow though the grief process. This learning helped me live more at ease with the uncertain future in all areas of my life. I believe this experience of grieving my father contributed to the courage it took to quit my job and step into the UNKNOWN after the stock market crashed. I believe the message that day of EMBRACE THE UNKNOWN WITH CERTAINTY was my father encouraging me to remember the internal strength I had developed, and to step into the unknown future without hesitation or fear. I have found in my work that fear of possible loss (Worry Habit) is a thinking pattern that can keep you trapped and diminish every area of your life.

As you challenge your BELIEFS you will realize that the energy in the present day is filled with creative opportunity for you. You will miss out if you hold onto the BELIEF that the only option that exists is that YOUR past will only re-create more of the same. The past CREATES NOTHING in the present day, unless you bring the negative energy with you in your thinking. The actual events are over. Your past is happening in your thinking, if you CHOOSE to recreate the negative emotional energy. **Creative life will never be found in the past**. DO NOT emotionally live in the past. Do not accept YOUR belief that you are destined to keep re-creating your mistakes. The present moment is for CREATING TODAY, not re-creating and reliving the past.

Bring the learning from your past into the present day. More learning and less blaming of self and others changes the energy you are generating in your life in a very dramatic way. If you were meant to live in the stagnant energy of yesterday, you would not be given a NEW DAY. INTERNAL WISDOM is already in you awaiting your acceptance. By taking one small CORRECTIVE ACTION STEP, you are CREATING something new, NOW! Keep repeating your CORRECTIVE ACTION STEP until you **EMOTIONALLY OWN** the learning! **EMOTIONALLY OWNING** the learning means that you will easily repeat the new behavior in the future without even thinking about it. The new behavior will easily flow out with no effort on your part. **You now EMOTIONALLY OWN the change.**

<u>Where are you emotionally living?</u>

YESTERDAY - TODAY - TOMORROW

1. Do you see yourself with options and opportunities TODAY to have a CORRECTIVE EXPERIENCE?

2. Have you closed the door of potential change by believing the past MUST be repeated today?

3. Do you keep recreating your past out of fear of taking a risk by trusting your INTERNAL WISDOM and trying something new?

80

STUFF will never heal your past. *STUFF* will never fill the void. *STUFF* will never resolve internal pain and fears. *STUFF* will never quiet the "less than" voices.

Why have so much STUFF?

(Inherent Value)

*MARIANNE, your needing to be **RIGHT** and make her **WRONG** is causing <u>YOU</u> suffering.*

(Overhelping)

11

EMOTIONAL MATURITY

EMOTIONAL MATURITY is not a by-product of chronological age. **Identify where your level of EMOTIONAL MATURITY is by observing how you respond to the outcome of YOUR decisions.** Your EMOTIONAL MATURITY impacts your daily CHOICES and DECISIONS, which are the building blocks of your life. EMOTIONAL MATURITY develops as you CONTINUALLY accept that YOU are responsible for the positive and negative outcomes of your decisions. Whether the outcome is positive or negative you accept that YOU are the one who originated the energy. You are responsible for the outcome. **You do not have to like the outcome, but you ACCEPT that it is the direct result of YOUR choice.** EMOTIONAL MATURITY is staying on your own PATH by working towards your goals, and not being distracted by the external opinions of others. The behaviors of OVERGIVING, OVERHELPING and being out on FAIRNESS PATROL are all ways you can be distracted from keeping the focus on your own life/ path.

EMOTIONAL MATURITY is when you are willing to take the risk and work towards change. You know that if you make a mistake, it is an EXTERNAL problem to resolve, not a negative value judgment about yourself. By not personalizing mistakes you are able to learn and change. EMOTIONAL MATURITY is learning to sustain your own motivation to follow through with goals, without constant external pressure. EMOTIONAL MATURITY understands that by letting go of past resentments, your energy flows towards your present day and future victories. You understand that YOU have a CHOICE where your energy is directed. EMOTIONAL MATURITY is saying "NO" to yourself and being willing to put off the quick fix, in pursuit of long term achievement. An EMOTIONALLY MATURE person ACCEPTS that he/she is creating his/her life by the power of each CHOICE and DECISION.

Emotional immaturity always wants to hear the answer "YES." Emotional immaturity is when the outcome of a decision is negative and is a DIRECT RESULT of your choice, you BELIEVE someone else is responsible or at fault. Emotional immaturity resolves INTERNAL emotional issues by EXTERNAL quick fixes such as changing jobs, relationships or using the geographical cure of moving to another state. Emotional immaturity sees mistakes as a negative value judgment on self, not an opportunity to learn. Emotional immaturity seeks continual EXTERNAL validation to sustain INTERNAL motivation. Emotional immaturity blames other people for the negative consequences of your choices, without seeing yourself as the original cause.

Emotional immaturity believes you can make a CHOICE and DECISION, and act that choice into your life without being responsible for the outcome, good or bad. You incorrectly believe someone else needed to have done it differently in the past, or in the future, for the situation to work out positively for you. This is the emotional approach you took as a child. You see the second action (the outcome or consequence), not YOUR ORIGINAL ACTION as the problem. You believe your boss, spouse, legal system are the problem, not YOUR ORIGINAL CHOICE and DECISION. The energy of your resentment has you living emotionally in the past. EMOTIONAL IMMATURITY negates all of YOUR power to create in the present day, by stoking the fire of resentment and shifting the blame onto others.

If you ask a child why he did something he was told not to do, he replies, "Because I felt like it." When you ask a child why he did not take care of something he was asked to do he might say, "I didn't feel like it." If you ask an adolescent why she did something she was told not to do, she will give you a dismissive look saying, "Because I felt like it." When you ask an adolescent why she did not take care of something she was asked to do, she will probably not look up from her phone and she will mumble, "I didn't feel like it." When the phone is taken away as a consequence of either doing or not doing what she was asked to do, she will say "my parents suck." She thinks the SECOND ACTION by her parents (taking the phone away as a consequence) is the ORIGINATION OF HER EMOTIONAL DISTRESS, not HER FIRST ACTION. Children and adolescents hear the "NO" as something negative. They feel the immediate disappointment, but do not see the bigger picture. Children and adolescents always want to hear the answer "YES" to any thing they desire in that moment, DESPITE what action they did or did not take.

By applying consequences parents are guiding the child and adolescent to an understanding that there are outcomes to the CHOICES and DECISIONS they make. Children and adolescents don't see any other way to behave other than their self-focused way of experiencing the world around them. Their level of EMOTIONAL MATURITY is, I do something or I don't do something according to WHAT "I" WANT to do at that moment. In adulthood, you no longer have the guiding energy of your parents and need to look to yourself. An impulsive, self centered, "It is all about me" approach needs to be outgrown. **You need to accept that YOUR consistent CHOICES and DECISIONS are creating YOUR life.**

If you want to develop EMOTIONAL MATURITY you can no longer use this mindset. The answer to the question of what is motivating YOUR decision today is no longer IF YOU WANT TO DO SOMETHING. The two questions you need to ask yourself now are: IS THIS SOMETHING I AM RESPONSIBLE TO DO? IS THIS SOMETHING I AM RESPONSIBLE NOT TO DO? Asking yourself if you WANT to do something or not is no longer your PRIMARY motivation. What is **MY RESPONSIBILITY NOW** is the only relevant question you need to ask yourself and answer. Your relationships, work, and self care will be continually impacted by how you answer these questions.

Seeking EXTERNAL comfort by always saying "YES" makes you vulnerable, because EXTERNAL events are easily disrupted. A sure sign you are looking towards EXTERNAL comfort is when you are Yes-Yes-Yesing yourself by looking for a QUICK FIX to ease emotional pain. This dynamic only increases your fear and anxiety, when you realize the emotional relief does not last. You may try to regain your feeling of comfort by attempting to control external events, and revert to old behaviors. Unfortunately, when you say "YES" to past habitual behaviors, the message you are repeatedly sending to yourself is that you deserve the negative consequences that you have experienced in the past. Making an impulsive decision can unintentionally bring the energy of your past into the present day. PAUSING can lead to a very different decision. Instead, work to keep your focus on the present, and what you would like to be creating NOW.

Saying "NO" to repeating past HABITUAL behaviors sends the message that you are WORTH something new, that you are WORTH all options that are now available. Learning to tell yourself "NO" is a major ingredient in EMOTIONAL MATURITY, because you accept that there are outcomes to the decisions you are making each day. "NO" for an adult is seeing past the immediate, impulsive, momentary quick fix, to appreciating the bigger picture of how you want to feel about yourself. "NO" helps you push past seeing the immediate EXTERNAL quick fix as being most important. You now experience peace and confidence within yourself. "NO" bypasses your need for immediate gratification, to experience the peace YOU have created in your INTERNAL world about yourself. Pause and ask yourself, is this decision replicating my past? Do I want to have a different experience by making a different decision?

EMOTIONAL MATURITY develops INTERNAL confidence, peace, and ease about yourself that is not disrupted by ANY external event. When you are at peace with yourself, external events can never challenge this feeling. You may be upset about an external event, but you remain at peace with yourself, as you work through the external problem and remain on YOUR PATH. This dynamic allows for the all important LEARNING OPPORTUNITY that is essential for your emotional growth. **Leaning to trust yourself and your decisions develops the INTERNAL confidence and comfort many people keep seeking EXTERNALLY.** Often people say they can not be happy with themselves, until external events are perfect. External events are often out of your control. How you feel about yourself each day is within your TOTAL control. Saying "NO" to yourself is a gift. Why would you not take advantage of such a powerful gift?

Recognizing the BENEFITS of saying "NO" to repeating old habitual behaviors is very important. You may still be emotionally experiencing "NO" as negative and yes as positive. When you say "NO" to yourself and keep this commitment, you are now sending out YOUR energy in a different direction from the SELF CREATED CHAOS routine of your past. Saying "NO" opens YOUR world to every new possibility and option. A new path is now open because anything is now possible. You NOW have expanded areas to grow and develop self confidence, and demonstrate that you are willing to try something new. **Learn to emotionally experience UNCERTAINTY and CHANGE as a gift, by realizing it offers the opportunity to trust your INTERNAL WISDOM and expand your life.** Saying "NO" for something you EXTERNALLY want will be to your benefit, as long as you work through the experience, and walk away with what you were meant to learn. The fresh energy of new opportunities is all yours when you commit to your "NO," because you are leaving your SELF CREATED CHAOS behaviors in the past.

Even though you can not see the end result, the original "NO" sends out the energy of compassion and self care. You have CHOSEN not to take the HABITUAL path that has led to SELF CREATED CHAOS opportunities in the past. **No matter the EXTERNAL reality, you can experience feeling at peace with yourself.** Isn't that really what you have wanted all along? Your

"NO" moves you in this direction and builds EMOTIONAL MATURITY and confidence. If you believe you have no choice other than to wait for people-places-situations external to yourself to change before you can be at peace with yourself, you will have a long wait. You have NO CONTROL OVER other people and what they will or will not do. You can emotionally experience yourself as a victim without realizing it. THERE IS NO POWER IN VICTIMHOOD that has been directly created by your CHOICES and DECISIONS.

We can be victimized by the behavior of others, when we are the recipient of the negative exchange of energy they have passed on to us. When we are the SECOND part of the exchange of energy, we are not the one responsible for the original energy. We are indeed responsible for how we respond, but we are not responsible for the original harm that was done. That is not the dynamic that I am referring to.

I am referring to when YOU make the original CHOICE, AND ACT THAT DECISION INTO YOUR LIFE. THE OUTCOME GOOD OR BAD BELONGS TO YOU. You seem to clearly accept this dynamic when the result is positive; yet when the result is negative, you can suddenly lose all reason and look for someone or something else to heap a big load of blame onto. You go around telling people about how unfairly you have been treated and how people, places and situations are doing you wrong. You are hoping someone else will collude with you and agree that YOU are not responsible, and you are a victim deserving of sympathy. When you tell YOUR VERSION OF THE STORY, you may be leaving out certain parts to make yourself seem not at all responsible. When you tell YOUR VERSION of the story over and over to yourself and others, it becomes MORE TRUE to you, but does not reflect the total reality. Reaching out to others to review your version of the event is your need to blame, without ever having to look at your own behavior. Note how may people you talk to about the issue. It will reflect how much you are deflecting responsibility.

As temporarily satisfying as deflecting personal responsibility may feel in the moment, there is one gigantic problem. When you feel it was the other person's fault, you believe you do not have to make changes in your own behavior, which keeps you trapped. You repeat your HABITUAL PATTERNS of behavior which yield the same results. By accepting your part and making CHANGES IN YOUR BEHAVIOR, you become powerful in your life. Waiting for everyone else to change is a helpless way to live. Practice building the skill of developing EMOTIONAL MATURITY when you are tempted to blame by keeping the focus on yourself. Take a powerful pause, breathe deeply. This brings you into the power of the present moment, opening the door to your INTERNAL WISDOM.

When you are upset about an outcome, ask yourself the following questions:

WHO TOOK THE FIRST ACTION?

Was I the one who took the first action and sent MY ENERGY OUT INTO THE WORLD?

Do I want to receive the energy back (outcome - consequence) I sent out?

If you took an ACTION STEP but don't want the energy back you sent out, don't waste your time making calls and sending all the texts for support. **Seeking external validation through blaming behaviors is useless to your learning.** If you identify that you took the first action that led to a negative outcome, offer yourself compassion. See it as an opportunity for learning humility. Own your part, apologize, and make a different choice in the future.

Accepting responsibly and making an apology is an important self care skill to develop. Accepting responsibility does not include needing to condemn yourself for making a mistake. Taking responsibility for your part is all you are required to do. Apologizing does not include pointing out what you feel the fault is with the other person (Overhelping). **Fault finding will not resolve any issue.** Have the courage to look at your part, without feeling the need to simultaneously point out the fault in the other person. See mistakes and feedback as learning opportunities. Be willing to hear and consider what is being said to you.

Holding yourself accountable for your part might sound like; "I was thinking about my part in this issue and can see I need to work on my anger and make changes." "This is on me and is unacceptable behavior I need to work on." Remember what you learned in the situation, and how you can apply the new learning in the future. This is very different from saying, I am sorry for the one hundredth time for blowing up, with really no intention to change the unacceptable behavior in the future.

When you set an INTENTION by stating, "I know I need to work on this behavior, I know this behavior is on me" and not blame the other person, you are setting an INTENTION of holding yourself accountable for this exact behavior in the future. It is not so easy to slide back into old patterns of behavior when you clearly state you know what you are doing is not respectful, and you intend to make a change. In the future, not keeping your word to yourself and others is an emotionally painful feeling. It will be much harder to use your old excuses to justify and rationalize your behavior, when you set an INTENTION of personal responsibility today. Look forward to your next opportunity for learning, as there will be many. That is what the human experience is all about. Then move it along, as I like to say, no need to emotionally dwell in the past.

I want to do what I want to do when I want to do it and no one is going to tell me otherwise. This is the emotional maturity of children and adolescents. We can find it amusing when children and adolescents act in this manner. However, any one who wants to be in a relationship with an emotionally mature adult, especially if they want to raise a family together, will hardly find this type of behavior amusing. Work environments do not applaud this type of behavior from an employee. They hired an adult and they expect adult choices and behaviors. Indeed, we can all have occasions when we act like a child. To have a life you would like to be living and feel powerful in your ability to create what you want, you can't remain an emotional child. This will only lead you back to the "quick fix" of projecting blame, which as I mentioned earlier will NEVER work to your advantage.

If you are interested to know if you are someone who primarily takes responsibility for the outcome of your choices, or if you deflect responsibility by blame, summon the courage to ask the people you live with for feedback. They will tell you very easily what you may not be able to see, or acknowledge in yourself. Possibly they already have. This step can be very challenging. It is well worth taking the risk, when you really want to learn and make changes to improve your life. If someone loves you enough to answer the question honestly, think about what they have said. Ask yourself again, "What can I learn in this situation?" This keeps the focus on you.

I used this approach myself when I was first out of school and started working on a psychiatric unit. I became aware in staff meetings that I was often becoming frustrated with the response of others. There was a women in the staff meeting whom I respected, so I began to ask her after the meeting how I was coming across. I asked for her opinion many times and she respected me enough to offer honest feedback. Yes, it did sting and bruise the ego, but the feedback has been tremendously beneficial. The piece of wisdom I remember most and utilize to this day is, "Marianne, when you say something once, you have been very clear, there is no need to repeat yourself." She was exactly correct. I am very clear and direct when I speak, but when I repeat, repeat and repeat myself it is because I am angry that I did not get my way. I kept repeating myself feeling frustrated that others did not understand my point. The reality was that I was increasingly frustrated because **I was not getting my own way**. Changing this dynamic has had significant benefits in many areas of my life. My friend saw the immaturity in my behavior and helped me by clearly and compassionately sharing her wisdom. We were friends for many years, until she passed from cancer.

Taking responsibly for your decisions allows you to build confidence in your ability to learn, no matter the situation. You build confidence in trusting your INTERNAL WISDOM. Learning to trust your choices and decisions is an invaluable gift that YOU can only give to yourself. No one else can do it for you. Only YOU can expand your level of EMOTIONAL MATURITY. Endlessly looking for someone else to fulfill this role is impossible. No one else can do your emotional internal work, because no one else knows what is best for you. You alone have access to your INTERNAL WISDOM, and only you can apply it to your life. Trusting yourself and building YOUR life one choice and decision at a time is your work.

Life is really not that complicated. When you are feeling that your life is way out of balance, you can believe that you must take **drastic action** to get back on track. This belief often feels impossible and so FIX ME FATIGUE sets in, and you lose all energy for change. Instead of believing that drastic measures must be taken all at once, believe that one simple "NO" can change your direction. Simply put, saying "NO" to yourself is an important self care tool. Saying "NO" to yourself and others directs you back to the basics of self care, and changes the energy on YOUR PATH . Self care is a personal process, so explore what is best for YOU. To avoid the regret of an impulsive decision, ask yourself:

1. How old emotionally is the person who will be making the decision I am considering right now? Is it a child, adolescent or an adult?

2. How old is the person who made the decision that I regret?

3. If you asked for feedback, how emotionally old are you when you are hearing the feedback? Is it a child, adolescent or an adult?

4. What is your emotional reaction when you hear "NO."

*What are **YOUR** thoughts forming? Do you want what **YOUR** thoughts are forming? Simply look around the landscape of **YOUR** life to answer these questions!*

(Thought Cascade)

I *unshackle myself from needing to be* **RIGHT**.

MY *needing to be* **RIGHT** *creates such suffering in me.*

(Emotional Maturity)

12

THOUGHT CASCADE

A REACTIVE NEGATIVE FIRST THOUGHT to an external problem may trigger a NEGATIVE THOUGHT CASCADE which can result in an impulsive decision. A NEGATIVE THOUGHT CASCADE sounds like; I didn't get the job – I am too old – no one else is going to hire me – that proves I will NEVER get ANY job - I'm a loser - I feel so depressed. One negative thought leads to another negative thought, triggering painful emotions. A REACTIVE NEGATIVE FIRST THOUGHT is often triggered by fearful energy from YOUR past, or fearful energy YOU are projecting into the future. **The emotional cascade that follows can lead to an impulsive choice to numb your feelings**. It is important to identify a REACTIVE NEGATIVE FIRST THOUGHT to avoid an impulsive action. Your goal is to pause, identify, objectively observe, and then challenge the REACTIVE NEGATIVE FIRST THOUGHT.

Why is it important to identify NEGATIVE self talk or NEGATIVE internal voices? You are consciously and subconsciously creating EACH DAY what you feel you deserve. Don't let your REACTIVE NEGATIVE FIRST THOUGHT of feeling "less than" trigger an impulsive decision today. If you allow the THOUGHT CASCADE to remain unchallenged, you ride the negative thinking pattern to emotional pain and self loathing. **NOW, your CHOICES will match**

someone who feels they are "less than," resulting in repeating your past self sabotaging behaviors (Self Created Chaos). If you are struggling today with negative self talk (self critical internal voices), you have a wonderful LEARNING OPPORTUNITY to make changes in how you view yourself (Inherent Value). When you value yourself, your CHOICES and DECISIONS are impacted by your beliefs, and usually reflect an improved outcome.

You can be unknowingly triggering a NEGATIVE THOUGHT CASCADE when you do not identify YOUR historical self critical internal voice. Your self critical internal voice is often historical negative energy re-emerging from YOUR past. This negative energy colors how you view and emotionally experience your life today. Your REACTIVE NEGATIVE FIRST THOUGHT (self critical internal voice) is replaying your old fears, self condemning voices, or scary stories. The voice can be with you on a daily basis or re-emerge when you least expect it. These thoughts can be your voice or the voices of others, who have burdened you with their OWN self critical voice. You are shutting down all options for CHANGE, when you react in the present day from historical energy or thinking patterns of YOUR past. You simply repeat old self sabotaging behaviors (Self Created Chaos). It is imperative when you are experiencing negative feelings towards yourself or a situation, that you identify your NEGATIVE FIRST THOUGHT and OBJECTIVELY observe and CHALLENGE it.

Learning to identify and move past the REACTIVE NEGATIVE FIRST THOUGHT is crucial. A REACTIVE NEGATIVE FIRST THOUGHT often goes unnoticed because you are feeling the intense painful EMOTIONAL REACTION to the thought. When you are experiencing painful feelings, you do not pause and challenge the first thought that triggered the distressing emotion to see if it is actually true. You focus on the painful emotional reaction, not the negative THOUGHT CASCADE that was the trigger. When something happens (external) that is upsetting or unexpected, your FIRST reactive thought can be negative or fearful in nature. Additional fearful thoughts will AUTOMATICALLY FOLLOW and will continue cascading in the same negative direction. This results in a painful emotional reaction which is what you focus on.

Observe the thought, but don't water and fertilize it with follow up negative thoughts, triggering an even more emotionally painful cascade. By training yourself to PAUSE and OBJECTIVELY observe the REACTIVE NEGATIVE FIRST THOUGHT you can prevent or redirect the THOUGHT CASCADE. You NOW have the opportunity to challenge the thought in the present moment, and redirect your SECOND THOUGHT in a more productive direction (Corrective Experience). It can help to write the thought down on a piece of paper and then list the emotions that are most painful. This step allows you to PAUSE and not just emotionally react to the situation. You can take a step back and evaluate if your painful emotional reaction is being triggered by YOUR own history. When you feel painful emotions, pause and identify YOUR thoughts. Are you interpreting the event through the energy of present day INHERENT VALUE or shame (past history)?

When you observe your REACTIVE NEGATIVE FIRST THOUGHT pause, and re-direct your thinking towards a CREATIVE THOUGHT CASCADE. Try saying; "Yes, that's a WORRY HABIT thought from the past/future." Give the thought NO power NOW by attaching an emotional response. You have taken a PAUSE and brought yourself into the present moment (I like to say learning moment). You have interrupted the NEGATIVE THOUGHT CASCADE and NOW have the option to replace it with a different thought, possibly your new mantra. A CREATIVE THOUGHT CASCADE will result in a very different emotional reaction. **You open yourself to unlimited options for resolving the problem, instead of impulsively repeating past self sabotaging behaviors.**

Your **DELIBERATE** SECOND THOUGHT is your effort to re-set your thinking pattern towards a CREATIVE THOUGHT CASCADE (Setting Intention). When the **DELIBERATE** second thought is set in motion, the third and fourth thoughts and your emotional reaction will follow more easily in the same direction. Re-directing your second thought is not an attempt to look on the bright side. External problems are real, painful and can be challenging to resolve. Your **DELIBERATE** effort to re-direct your second thought prevents a painful emotional reaction based on a NEGATIVE FIRST THOUGHT, that probably was not even TRUE. **The action you NOW take will be following a PRESENT MOMENT decision on the path you most desire, and not down the familiar painful path of your past.**

You can always challenge a negative THOUGHT CASCADE at any time, even if you are into your tenth negative thought and feel despairing. It is best to try and catch the FIRST thought, but if not, it is never too late. Challenging a REACTIVE NEGATIVE FIRST THOUGHT the next day is possible, even after feeling anxious and depressed all night. Good, you have noticed the problem NOW and challenged it. Great! You can remind yourself that you are learning and trying to do your best. This re-focus in thought can lead to a more compassionate feeling about yourself. The energy of self compassion results in a different emotional reaction and ACTION STEP. This offers you the opportunity to NOW make a choice based on self compassion, instead of a habitual REACTIVE response of self loathing. It is easy to see how having a habitual thought pattern of self loathing or self compassion leads to very different decisions and ACTION STEPS.

When you do not challenge your "I am less than" thinking pattern (Inherent Value), you can IMMEDIATELY begin to beat yourself up for EVEN HAVING THE THOUGHT. When you notice an "I am less than" thought pop up and react with a JUDGMENTAL second thought, you trigger a THOUGHT CASCADE leading to more emotional suffering. If you have ever had this experience you know that when your thoughts are self condemning, you experience a painful emotional response. As a general rule (historically), YOUR emotional reaction at the end of an "I am less than" THOUGHT CASCADE is .... (fill in the blank)!

If you allow YOUR negative THOUGHT CASCADE (self critical internal voice) from the past to impact YOUR present day decisions, it will become more emotionally painful. These self critical thoughts and emotions will influence how you are going to resolve the present day issue. Instead of having the one problem to resolve, you are now up against an additional challenge, your old thinking patterns (self critical internal voice). This is why, even when you do not want to keep repeating your old behavioral patterns, you do. YOUR decisions are a reflection of how you TRULY feel about yourself. When you experience your mood being anxious-depressed-fearful-resentful-angry, pause and ask yourself, "What am I thinking about?"

YOUR decisions and actions build your experiences in life. This is important LEARNING and is well worth YOUR effort to practice. **Remember, even if the experience has been painful, you will move past ANY situation on the positive end, as long as there has been LEARNING**. Yes, it can take time and effort to CHOOSE to be so deliberate with your thinking pattern. When you realize the impact on your mood and your life, you will decide how much energy you are willing to give to the task. It takes repeated effort to pause, OBJECTIVELY observe and challenge YOUR thoughts. The significant energy initially needed to be deliberate with your SECOND THOUGHT, will become routine and eventually second nature with CONTINUED practice.

Your WILLINGNESS to practice self care will naturally generate a more compassionate energy towards yourself. PAUSING even for five seconds, taking a breath, and OBJECTIVELY observing the FIRST THOUGHT before you impulsively react, is an important skill in self care and requires diligence. You are COURSE CORRECTING and putting yourself on the PATH you wish to walk. Thinking and feeling I AM "LESS THAN" leads down one path. Thinking and feeling I HAVE INHERENT VALUE leads down another path. You are in control of what PATH you are walking on. It ALL starts in your thinking! Water and fertilize the thoughts you want to expand and grow. The weeds (Negative Thoughts) will die away when they are not watered and fed by a NEGATIVE THOUGHT CASCADE. What are the thoughts YOU are using to water your emotional garden?

Are you watering with more guilt or forgiveness? Are you watering with more anxiety or peace? Are you watering with more shame or inherent value? Are you watering with more resentment or forgiveness? Are you watering with more fear or courage? Are you watering with more scary stories or your new mantra? Are you watering with more past regrets or mindful moments?

How to re-direct a REACTIVE NEGATIVE FIRST THOUGHT

FIRST THOUGHT: "I'm a loser, I NEVER do anything right."

Pause: objectively observe it – write it down - challenge it.

SECOND THOUGHT: "What people say about me is true, I never do anything right."

(Re-direct: Yes, I didn't do my best on this one. Laziness got the best of me, but I am not giving up.)

THIRD THOUGHT: "It never goes right for me, why keep trying."

(Re-direct: Yes, I have made my mistakes, but I have set an INTENTION to be more responsible and have been living up to my INTENTION the best way I know how.)

FOURTH THOUGHT: "That drink-drug-scratch ticket-chocolate will fix it."

(Re-Direct: Looking at the bigger picture goal (Intention) compared to this time last year, I actually have been much more responsible. Not perfect, but moving in the direction I want to go.)

YOUR EMOTIONAL REACTION

CREATIVE THOUGHT CASCADE **(Re-direct)**	*NEGATIVE THOUGHT CASCADE*
Slight disappointment in myself	Self loathing - shame
MOTIVATED to continue with my goals	Despair
No emotional energy to punish or self sabotage	Anxiety- depression- anger
Practicing self care through compassion	Inaction

1. When you water your garden, do you water and fertilize the flowers (CREATIVE THOUGHT CASCADE) or the weeds (NEGATIVE THOUGHT CASCADE)?

2. Ask yourself; do my thoughts cascade more towards fear/anxiety/limitation/depression or INHERENT VALUE and learning?

3. Start a CREATIVE THOUGHT CASCADE.

I am grateful for ....

What is the result of a negative THOUGHT CASCADE?

A negative Emotional/Feeling Cascade.

What is a negative Emotional/Feeling Cascade?

Imagine the power of an emotionally painful Niagara Falls.

(Worry Habit)

*It is only in laying down **MY** emotional weapons of judgment, anger, hate, resentment, bitterness and regret towards others that **I** can LIVE a life of **JOY** and **EASE**. I cannot have both, because they are opposing energies. Lay down your emotional weapons towards **yourself** as well.*

(Compassion or Judgment)

13

COMPASSION or *JUDGMENT*

Amazingly, YOU fear being judged by OTHERS, when it is YOUR behavior of judging OTHERS that is hurting you most. It is YOUR OWN actions that are causing you emotional pain. YOUR need to judge another person is a projection of fear about yourself. When you judge, you think it is the other person who is causing you distress. Your judgments are never a reflection of the other person. **YOUR need to judge is simply a reflection of YOU and how you feel about yourself.**

Holding a primary belief of feeling "LESS THAN" is a breeding ground for the "quick fix" of judging others. You TEMPORARILY feel better about yourself. Judging others helps you feel "superior" or "better than, " yet this is a short-lived fix. The eventual fall from feeling "better than" to crashing back into the quicksand of feeling "LESS THAN" is a painful emotional experience. To avoid these painful emotions, you just KEEP ON JUDGING.

Judging is a LEARNED HABIT. It is so much easier to break this LEARNED HABIT of JUDGING with the energy of COMPASSION towards yourself and others. Have you ever judged others only to find yourself doing the exact same thing some time in the future? Now, the judgmental energy you had heaped onto others is the same judgmental energy YOU will have to face about yourself. An example of this dynamic is how we often feel about other people who are charged with Driving Under the Influence. As part of my work, I facilitated First and Second Offender Groups for those who were convicted of Driving Under the Influence. Most people came into the group shocked that THEY were now a "drunk driver." People would feel such shame and often not even tell their own families.

Before they were standing in front of the judge, they saw themselves differently from "THOSE PEOPLE" whom they had negatively judged in the past. Their JUDGEMENT of others blinded them from realizing and accepting the reality of their own behavior. When they saw the blue lights behind them on the day they were arrested, they wished they had made a different choice. Group members would come to understand that although they had been drinking and driving for many years, they never saw themselves as a drunk driver. **Their negative judgements of others blinded them to the truth about their own behavior. Eventually, they were able to acknowledge that they had been drinking and driving for many years**. They were judging other people for drinking and driving while engaging in the SAME behavior.

Resisting your HABIT of judging is not about condoning behavior. It is simply finding COMPASSION for another human being who has made a mistake. WORK (yes it can be work) to offer COMPASSION instead of judging yourself and others, but it is worth the effort. You may notice in the future that when YOU are the one who has made the mistake, you may not instantaneously jump to YOUR old thinking patterns of being harsh and judging yourself without mercy. **You will NEVER learn from wallowing in the energy of self condemnation.** Instead, feed YOURSELF thoughts and feelings of COMPASSION. It may feel uncomfortable at first, and feel like you are 'force feeding" yourself compassion. Do it anyway. Self COMPASSION allows you to learn from your mistakes, with the hope of handling life differently in the future. **There is NO learning or emotional growth in the energy of judging yourself or others.**

Have you ever noticed that you can have far more COMPASSION for others than you have for yourself? It can be challenging at times to live a life of COMPASSION. Is it worth your effort? Notice in a twenty-four hour period of time how often your thoughts are focused on judging others. You may notice you spend a similar amount of time or more judging yourself. When you work on not judging others, you may notice that you judge yourself much less. The judgmental energy you give out is the same energy you will have to face yourself. You are the one generating the energy. Do you want judgmental energy or COMPASSIONATE energy for yourself?

COMPASSION is the energy that dissolves the toxic effects of judging, not only for the other person, but most importantly for yourself. Offering compassion instead of judging yourself and others is a great lesson in the exchange of LOVE ENERGY. The energy you give out, you will receive back. If you want evidence regarding the kind of energy you are emitting, simply feel the energy you are CONSISTENTLY receiving back from others. Question answered.

1. How would YOUR day be different if you made it a priority to lead with COMPASSION towards yourself and others?

2. What would you be doing differently?

3. How would you be feeling about YOURSELF at the end of the day?

*Every time **I** make the decision to take extraordinary care of myself and stay on my own PATH, **I** am MEETING my authentic soul - so **I** can meet ME as often as **I** want today.*

(Inherent Value)

The outside world can be a tsunami, but you can remain at peace with you. Yes, the outside world can be a problem, but don't lose the ease within yourself. **Your peace with YOU remains peace, no matter the outside world.**

(My Path)

14

SELF CREATED CHAOS

SELF CREATED CHAOS is a pattern of self sabotaging behaviors. **Your motivation for creating chaos is not because it feels good, but because it feels FAMILIAR and SAFE.** You know how to behave and what to expect in your old patterns of behavior. You may create chaos deliberately or out of habit. Making a different choice by taking a new ACTION STEP may be fear provoking. Instead, you consciously or subconsciously search out SELF CREATED CHAOS opportunities that feel FAMILIAR and far less scary. You have been here before, and know just what it will feel like to be embroiled in past habitual behaviors. You know your place in SELF CREATED CHAOS. You have played this role many times before to avoid the emotional discomfort of CHANGE and UNCERTAINTY. You do have the POWER to create, and sometimes you create a familiar conflict to avoid the emotional risk of trying something new.

External improvements do not always equate to feeling emotionally peaceful with yourself. It may actually increase your anxiety when EXTERNAL things begin to improve. When others see positive external changes, you may feel more pressure to live up to their expectations. You may resent feeling additional responsibilities. It is uncomfortable when you and others see your external world improving, but your "less than" (self critical voice) continues to scream. You feel emotionally off balance because YOU do not feel that you deserve improvement in your life, even when you have been working hard toward change. **BELIEVING you "DO NOT DESERVE" the beneficial changes that are happening in your life is a painful emotional experience.** Sabotaging by SELF CREATED CHAOS is one way to return to feeling balanced on the outside (external) as well as on the inside. It does not feel good, but it does feel FAMILIAR and SAFE.

Facing CHANGE and UNCERTAINTY requires emotional courage. Building this courage takes time and practice. It can feel like stepping out of a boat in the middle of a lake when you can't swim and have no life preserver. Why take the risk? You take the risk to build confidence in your ability to "swim" and create what you want in life. Every time you take a new ACTION STEP by jumping out of the boat (make a change), you build confidence in your ability to emotionally manage your life. **Emotionally growing and learning over time by risking taking a new ACTION STEP, allows you to build confidence in YOURSELF and feel more comfortable with CHANGE and UNCERTAINTY.** Building confidence to handle anything that happens in your life makes it easier to step out of the boat whenever you need to make a change. Each time you jump out of the boat and learn, it will become easier. Simply being alive involves continual CHANGE and UNCERTAINTY. Engaging in new behaviors will promote emotional growth and expand YOUR opportunities and options. Are you willing to take the risk to learn (step out of your boat)?

The emotional view from YOUR boat (life) can be clouded with the fog of fear-anger-depression-anxiety-addiction-illness-resentment. When you are EXPECTING THE WORST (Worry Habit), you can be stunned to realize after you take the FIRST ACTION STEP (step out of the boat), you were ALREADY on dry land. **You AVOIDED making a CHANGE for so long out of fear of sinking to the bottom (making a mistake), only to realize that what you feared was not even true.** Even if your boat does feel adrift, you may one day be shocked to realize that you can actually "walk on water" and CREATE what you felt was impossible. (Writing this book is a good example.) You must take the risk of an ACTION STEP.

When you risk taking a new ACTION STEP and experience the emotional benefit, you will eventually realize that staying IN the boat is what is causing the fear/anxiety/pain. Humans are created with the innate ability to CHANGE, LEARN and GROW. It is NOT your fear of CHANGE and UNCERTAINTY that is the problem. These beliefs/feelings are overcome by stepping out of the boat and experiencing the adrenaline rush of taking an ACTION STEP to learn something new. **What is causing the unrelenting despair is NOT CHANGING.** You want to stay safe in your comfort zone or what I like to call the BOREDOM ZONE. NOT CHANGING (never stepping out of the boat) over days, weeks, months, years of your life leads to emotional stagnation. You can remain in the boat and initially feel safe, but there is no growing or expanding in your life. Emotional stagnation is usually the outcome. Stagnation goes against the natural order of nature and results in decay. Emotional stagnation is a painful place to exist. It is the opposite of FULLY LIVING.

When you risk stepping out of the boat (make a change) it does not matter if you "walk on water" or sink to the bottom (make a mistake) as we ALL do. You are building confidence in your ability to make it to the shore. Making it to the shore does not mean safety. It means learning from mistakes with the INTENTION of doing it differently in the future. When mistakes are made, you can always make it to the shore by asking yourself, "What is my learning," and setting an INTENTION for a different outcome in the future. **When the CHANGE is UNEXPECTED and not part of your plan, remind yourself that you do not have to like the change, but are you willing to emotionally grow and learn through it?**

FULLY LIVING involves making changes and risking mistakes. Experience your mistakes as wonderful LEARNING OPPORTUNITIES. Your mistakes do not call for punishment. **You are not condemned to treat yourself poorly in the present day because of your past mistakes, unless you make the CHOICE to do so.** Others have no right to treat you poorly due to your mistakes. A major TRAP in your thinking is that you believe you cannot have what you desire in life today, or in the future, because of your past mistakes. Since you cannot change the past, you believe you are destined to keep repeating old patterns of behavior. You change your emotional experience of feeling trapped by observing your thinking pattern and becoming aware of your primary BELIEFS and challenging the NEGATIVE thoughts. You always have an option.

It is an interesting dynamic that when YOU have worked hard to make changes and EXTERNAL situations in YOUR life begin to improve, YOU sometimes notice a disquieting internal feeling. When you emotionally have an INTERNAL "less than" feeling about yourself AND events in your EXTERNAL life are negative this dynamic feels familiar, not good, but familiar. **When people continue to feel "less than" and EXTERNAL events greatly IMPROVE, there is an emotional disconnect between INTERNAL painful emotions and positive EXTERNAL reality.** This imbalance triggers uncomfortable feelings, because your EXTERNAL world and INTERNAL world (how you feel about yourself) are not emotionally matching.

Although the feeling is uncomfortable, it is important to recognize that this is your INTERNAL WISDOM speaking to you. Your INTERNAL WISDOM is sending you a life changing message. What the disquieting energy is telling you is that you are working on the outside STUFF, instead of working on how you feel about yourself. You are not honoring your INHERENT VALUE. You are making the mistake of believing that EXTERNAL STUFF or accomplishments will heal the "less than" painful feelings. Eventually you realize that acquiring EXTERNAL STUFF does not ease your emotional pain. Unfortunately, a common response to this disquieting feeling is to return to a familiar pattern of SELF CREATED CHAOS. These old patterns of behavior often involve numbing feelings. **When you numb your feelings, YOU have lost connection to your INTERNAL WISDOM and will learn very little in the current experience.** More than likely, you will repeat negative behavioral patterns of your past.

When you become aware of this emotionally uncomfortable disconnect, pause, and take time to honor and value how you feel. Then ask yourself, do I believe/feel that I deserve the EXTERNAL good that is happening? If you quickly answer "NO," be grateful you have recognized this negative thinking pattern, because you have just had a CORRECTIVE EXPERIENCE. Instead of impulsively returning to SELF CREATED CHAOS to numb the emotional pain, you listened to your INTERNAL WISDOM. You validated your uncomfortable feelings instead of negating them and can NOW address the issue. You have a choice on how to deal with the disquieting internal emotions. Your choice is to have a SELF CREATED CHAOS experience, or have a CORRECTIVE EXPERIENCE. You do this by taking a new ACTION STEP that honors your INHERENT VALUE. **You do not have to feel your INHERENT VALUE to take an ACTION STEP to improve your life. Do it anyway despite how you feel.** Take the ACTION STEP as many times as you need. Eventually, you will reconnect with your POWER.

Have the COURAGE to acknowledge that you have options. I say have the COURAGE, because options leave the door wide open for the potential for CHANGE. **Realizing CHANGE as an OPTION can increase your anxiety/fear.** Do NOT be bothered by this initial THOUGHT. Do not allow it to turn into a negative THOUGHT CASCADE and talk you out of your dream. It is not until the emotional pain of staying where you are (not stepping out of the boat/avoiding life) becomes GREATER than your anxiety about making a change, that you will DECIDE to get out of the boat. I have often wondered how I would be doing if I had not stepped out of the boat to leave my job after the stock market crashed. Well, you clearly would not be reading this book. I would be sitting in the boat decaying. Trust INTERNAL WISDOM.

1. Does your past dictate what your future must be?

2. Do you use the past as a way to avoid taking personal responsibly for what you are doing today?

3. What perspective are you seeing from at this exact moment in your life?

4. Are you viewing yourself from an emotional place of worth or from an emotional place of being "less than?"

5. How can you begin to challenge these distorted beliefs and make different choices in your current life?

6. Are you comfortable when your life is going well or does peace make you uncomfortable?

Expect it!

Expect It!

Expect it!

You CREATE what YOU expect!

*What are you EXPECTING
FOR YOURSELF today?*

(Thought Cascade)

*Set an **INTENTION** to walk towards acceptance of **personal responsibility** to the highest degree you are able.*

NOW, take an additional small step forward.

(Emotional Maturity)

15

I AM CHOOSING ...

YOU are making choices and decisions that are creating your daily life NOW. Telling yourself "I can't" have something you want may emotionally bring you back to childhood. You may react by acting out. Feelings of rebellion return. There is no POWER in saying "I can't," because saying "I can't" do something is not true. You can do it. You can have the drink-drug-food-scratch ticket and no one is going to stop you. You are an adult now, not a child. "I can't" may trigger an immature impulsive decision that is not in your best interest. YOU have the POWER of CHOICE. **Saying instead, "I AM CHOOSING" not to have the drink-drug-scratch ticket-food because of how I want to feel about myself is an empowering alternative.** The energy is being generated from a place of POWER because you are GAINING SOMETHING you want, feeling good about yourself.

Pause and play the choice through in your thinking pattern to the end (action-outcome-emotional consequence). If I make the SAME choice and act that choice into my life, how is it likely to end? Use your past experiences to answer the question. When you have long-held behaviors, you are well aware what the outcome will most likely be. However, you can engage in selective memory which focuses only on what you have enjoyed. You don't seem to recall the negative outcome that is attached to taking the SAME action. Do you want the outcome of this action again? If yes, then by all means take the action and accept the outcome as yours. If you do not want the same outcome, CHOOSE not to take the SAME action. Experience your POWER of CHOICE and DECISION.

Saying yes to repeating old behaviors, the child in you thinks you are "gaining" something. **What you are "gaining" are the consequences you have experienced many times in the past and usually do not want again.** You are offering yourself the opportunity to feel horrible again. You feel like you are actually losing something with the "I can't" mentality and act out by repeating past behaviors that are actually hurting you again. Unfortunately, feeling the quick fix of YES will ultimately end in a "NO" for you. You are really losing when you say YES to repeating old negative behaviors.

You are actually GAINING something when you CHOOSE not to take the same action. By changing your thinking pattern from "I can't" to "I AM CHOOSING," you are gaining a peaceful day with empowered feelings about yourself, and usually a better outcome. Choosing NOT to engage in emotionally numbing behaviors opens your life to expanded experiences. Saying "YES" to self defeating behaviors is returning to the emotional pain you have experienced in the past (Self Created Chaos). Saying "NO" to self defeating behaviors offers you unlimited opportunities to create something new, and feel good about yourself.

Emotionally numbing yourself is like buying a shovel, digging a hole, jumping in and shoveling the dirt back over your head. You thought you would feel safe being numb, when all you have done is emotionally trap yourself. **You have suffocated your life energy.** It is too late to realize that saying YES to engaging in the compulsive behaviors to numb your emotions did not resolve the problem. The original problem has not gone away and is still waiting for you after you dig yourself out of the hole. Buying the shovel is YOUR action of choice. Digging the hole is YOUR action of choice. Jumping in that hole is YOUR action of choice. Shoveling dirt on top of YOUR head is YOUR action of choice. Sitting in the dark with no air, blackness and despair is the outcome and consequence of YOUR CHOICE. Are you willing to change? How can you make a change in this pattern of behavior? Are you willing to CHOOSE not to take the first action that leads to despair? Are you willing to NOT BUY THE SHOVEL?

YOU CAN **"CHOOSE"** NOT TO BUY THE SHOVEL by challenging the original negative thought-craving urge and not engage in emotionally numbing behaviors. **You have the power to**

make a different choice. Not buying the shovel can be an action choice for the future. When you are experiencing emotional pain and want to numb your distressing feelings, saying "I can't" have the drink-drug-scratch ticket-food throws gasoline on the fire of your cravings and urges. The compulsion grows and burns more intensely. Engaging in compulsive behaviors for relief grows more frequent. Changing compulsive behaviors is a challenge, but it is possible.

There are outcomes to making a choice and putting the energy of your choice into the world. It does not matter if you like or do not like the outcome. You are the originator of the energy and responsible for the result. **THE ENERGY STARTED WITH YOU.** We all have patterns of behavior that increase our suffering and decrease our joy, happiness and contentment in life. You can change the outcome by changing YOUR CHOICE . This may involve taking a new ACTION STEP and moving out of your comfort zone (Boredom Zone), but it is an important step in honoring your INTENTION to make a change. **Changing YOUR energy by making a different decision instead of BLAMING is how you use YOUR power of CHOICE to create.**

Blaming starts from a place of fear. If you are unhappy with the outcome of something YOU have chosen, projecting the energy of blame onto others just doubles your emotional pain. You now have the original problem, along with experiencing anger and resentment waiting for people-places-situations to change before you can be happy. **Instead of taking the risk to make a different choice, you trap yourself in the mental quicksand of blaming others.** You avoid looking in the mirror and holding yourself accountable. YOUR projection of blame nullifies YOUR CREATIVE POWER of choice. **Blaming only increases YOUR fear.**

Fears are negative beliefs stuck in your thinking patterns. People can feel paralyzed by their fear of failing and making the wrong choice. They will not take one step forward out of fear of making the wrong decision and not being perfect. Perfectionism will not keep you safe, and believing that it will is emotional quicksand. You build confidence in yourself by making a decision, possibly failing but not giving up, making another decision and succeeding. This pattern is a formula for slowly building confidence. BELIEVING you are the only human being on the earth that is NEVER allowed to make a mistake is very destructive and limiting to your emotional growth. You build confidence when you overcome mistakes, and do not allow the fear of not being perfect to prevent you from even starting.

The opposite of making a decision and taking action is taking no action at all, or avoidance. You avoid taking action to put off what you feel may be emotionally difficult. Avoidance is a strategy to not have to address and resolve present day problems. You want the quick fix of protecting yourself, so you will not have to face the outcome of the choice. Unfortunately, you only kick the fear and anxiety down the road, where it will be WAITING for you at some future time. **The consequences of avoidance are that you NOW experience an increase in anxiety and fear, as well as having to deal with the original avoided issue.** (Not opening your mail for several months at a time to avoid dealing with your debt is a good example.) Avoidance increases your anxiety and fear. Regardless of your justification for not taking action on the issue and resolving it, your anxiety and preoccupation about the issue will only increase. You now become preoccupied with the painful feelings you were originally trying to avoid and ruin any enjoyment in YOUR day. Children shut their eyes and believe no one can see them. You can shut your eyes pretending there is no problem, only to be run down by a larger emotional issue sometime in the future **when you least expect it.** We can avoid dealing with difficult issues for many reasons:

"What if people get angry with me?"
"I don't want conflict."
"I don't want to hurt anyone's feelings."
"It needs to be perfect, if not I hate myself."
"I just don't feel like doing it."
"I hate change."
"I actually have no interest in being an adult today."
"It's hard, what if people start talking about me?"

You do not have to wait until something that is out of your control changes to experience peace. CONSISTENTLY accepting responsibility for the outcome of your CHOICES and DECISIONS allows you to be at peace, even when you make a mistake. Once you have failed, but not given up by pushing past YOUR uncomfortable emotions, you realize YOU really do have the power of creating what you want, especially how you feel about yourself. Your primary BELIEFS about yourself will impact your CHOICES and DECISIONS each day. Forgiving yourself and others for not being perfect is a powerful way to live in your own skin. This dynamic opens immediate access to your INTERNAL WISDOM.

Highlight the powerful energy you have within. Offer yourself the gift of feeling in control by remembering **YOUR POWER OF CHOICE.** Ease your emotional distress by responding with compassion, not judgment. Experiencing emotional relief as the painful energy passes will motivate you to continue with the new behavior. "I AM CHOOSING" not to take this action to numb my feelings will allow you to ride the wave of emotional pain, and get to the other side.

Prove it to YOURSELF by making the choice opposite of your past habitual behavior. You will emotionally experience walking right into YOUR POWER to CREATE. Keep practicing and experience the benefits of LEARNING, ACCEPTING and APPRECIATING **ALL** of your emotions.

When you are numbing your emotions you block access to your INTERNAL WISDOM, and wonder why you experience a void and feel so painfully alone in your life. Emotions are your guidance system for living. People can learn at an early age to fear emotions by numbing or acting out as a way to avoid painful feelings. You seek outside answers from others, rather than building trust in your ability to excel in life by trusting your INTERNAL WISDOM. **You gain confidence to manage your life when you listen for the guiding energy of your emotions and learn to create with them.** Taking an ACTION STEP to care for yourself develops expanded opportunities for emotional growth. **You begin to trust yourself and your ability to make creative decisions.**

TRUSTING YOURSELF IS PRICELESS

1. What feels more empowering to you; I can't or I AM CHOOSING....?

2. Does YOUR fear of failure impact how you make decisions? Identify where this fearful energy originated.

3. Ask yourself, is this THOUGHT a new fear?

4. Is this an old fear from childhood that has come back to visit me?

5. Is this my fear or the fear of someone else in my life?

117

Try changing "I can't" to "<u>I AM</u> CHOOSING" and feel the difference.

(I AM Choosing…)

I throw ALL my problems into Mother Nature's river and they just float away. I STAND steady in the river. The painful emotional ENERGY of what is no longer wanted or needed simply drifts away, provided I do not chase after it out of FEAR of CHANGE and UNCERTAINTY.

(Embrace the Unknown with Certainty)

16

EMOTIONAL MANIPULATION IS FEAR ENERGY

The hostile energy of EMOTIONALLY MANIPULATING others guarantees YOU emotional misery. You may get an emotional quick fix from achieving what you wanted, but all you have done is treat someone else as a "means to YOUR end." You are attempting to fix your own emotional issues (Inherent Value/fear) at the expense of someone else. You will NEVER feel in control of yourself by EMOTIONALLY MANIPULATING and attempting to control others. The hostile energy of EMOTIONAL MANIPULATION increases YOUR fear and results in YOUR feeling more out of control.

The emotional death spiral of EMOTIONAL MANIPULATION starts with YOUR feeling out of control or "less than." You attempt to control and EMOTIONALLY MANIPULATE people and events to cover these feelings. Other people do not do what you want. You feel more out of control and attempt to EMOTIONALLY MANIPULATE again, only to fail. Your fear, anxiety and "less than" voices increase. This dynamic will result in injuring your relationship. You were feeling bad enough about yourself, now you feel worse. You wonder why people keep leaving you, and really don't want to be around you.

EMOTIONAL MANIPULATION continues to generate MORE FEAR because it negatively impacts your most important relationships. EMOTIONALLY MANIPULATING others is a sure way to increase your own emotional suffering. You will always lose no matter how good a manipulator you feel you are today. **Your behavior of EMOTIONAL MANIPULATION is generated from YOUR energy of fear, never from a place of INTERNAL strength, worth or value.** YOU end up being alone or feeling alone, which validates your belief of being "less than."

Intimidating others from a place of fear keeps you emotionally on the outside of your relationships. You feel you are looking in on the relationship and not feeling a true emotional connection. You know others are walking on egg shells around you. How can there be any real honesty, if they hold back telling you their true feelings for fear of your angry reaction? The dynamic YOU are creating continues to keep you distant from any real honesty in the relationship. Is this what you want?

When you hold a primary BELIEF that you are "less than" it makes it very challenging to risk being vulnerable. **The irony is that YOU fear being rejected by others, when YOU are the one ALREADY rejecting yourself.** Experiencing an emotional barrier is painful and frustrating, when all YOU are really craving is genuine emotional connection. It is easy to say, "Just give up being an EMOTIONAL MANIPULATOR." However, when your fear is high and you feel out of control, feeling temporarily powerful and getting what you want through EMOTIONAL MANIPULATION can be a very hard HABIT to stop. YOU have the power to change.

EMOTIONAL MANIPULATION can be a challenging behavior to leave behind, especially when you appear to EXTERNALLY succeed in getting what you wanted in the moment. **The problem is that you will continue to fear you are going to lose what you manipulated for, because it does not emotionally belong to you.** What you did initially to DECREASE your fear and feel more in control, results in experiencing an INCREASE in fear and feeling more out of control. Unfortunately, YOUR emotional experience is the same, because the negative feelings INTERNALLY about yourself have not changed. The never ending cycle of EMOTIONAL MANIPULATION to decrease YOUR INTERNAL fear of being "less than" continues to fail.

Ask yourself, will the temporary feeling of "winning" by EMOTIONAL MANIPULATION be worth another swim in your pool of emotionally feeling unworthy and separate from others? Aren't you attempting to avoid these painful feelings in the first place? You may have a pretty cover (façade) over your "secret pool" of emotional unworthiness, but the cover is easily removed for another dip. The energy of EMOTIONAL MANIPULATION helps you dive right in. EMOTIONAL MANIPULATION will never quiet YOUR voice of feeling "less than." Your voice of fear will scream even louder. You are trapped by experiencing the exact emotional pain you were originally trying to avoid. **You probably do not realize that YOU are the one who is generating the increase in negative feelings through YOUR behavior of EMOTIONAL MANIPULATION.** BLAMING the other person or situation is a common reaction. Blaming results in not having to look at YOUR behavior as the trigger for YOUR increase in emotionally painful feelings (Emotional Maturity).

You can make the CHOICE not to do another lap in your emotional pool of misery. Make a choice to have a CORRECTIVE EXPERIENCE. The goal of a CORRECTIVE EXPERIENCE is to learn in the present day, by taking a new ACTION STEP in opposition to your past habitual behavior. You can take a step back and NOT put YOUR EMOTIONALLY MANIPULATIVE energy into the situation. Simply watch the CORRECTIVE ACTION unfold. "What! What do you mean, let it unfold?" I hear you screaming in protest. This may be scary and initially make you feel more fearful and out of control. These feelings are only temporary. **Learning how to tolerate uncomfortable feelings, going along for the ride, doing your best and letting the results take care of themselves opens a new tool for living.** You can prove it to yourself by taking an ACTION STEP towards what you want to create. This ACTION STEP will usually be in the opposite direction than you are accustomed to going. You must FEEL it work for you to BELIEVE in the emotional relief it will offer. Are you willing to take the leap and step out of YOUR boat?

The choice to not engage in EMOTIONALLY MANIPULATIVE behavior results in having a CORRECTIVE EXPERIENCE now. If you are willing to take the risk and not numb the pain, you emotionally experience what it feels like to overcome the original fear. Tolerating your emotional discomfort allows you to experience getting to the other side. Once there, you will experience emotional relief. Demonstrate you have the power to heal your emotional distress by making changes in YOUR BEHAVIOR. **No person, place or situation EXTERNAL to yourself needs to change or be controlled for you to feel at peace with yourself**. Although a situation may not end the way you want, you still have the opportunity to expand your skills by asking yourself, "WHAT IS MY LEARNING" during this time? What did I learn, and how can I bring this learning forward to improve my emotional experiences in the future?

Overtime CONTINUED PRACTICE of this skill will allow you to build confidence in yourself, and eliminate the HABIT of EMOTIONAL MANIPULATION for good. You will be enjoying genuine emotional connection in the present day. You will not want to give up this connection for the quick fix of EMOTIONAL MANIPULATION. Interfering in what is not your place to control creates much suffering for yourself and others (Overhelping). Life is so much more peaceful when you ultimately give up the hostile SELF CREATED CHAOS energy of EMOTIONAL MANIPULATION. **Remember, when you attempt to control people, places and situations by EMOTIONAL MANIPULATION, you only increase YOUR fear.**

YOU keep creating what you do not want, more FEAR.

1. Who are the people in your life you are most likely to manipulate?

2. Do you feel an emotional distance in your relationships when you emotionally manipulate?

3. Do you manipulate through the use of emotional blackmail by withholding love/approval?

4. Do you use physical intimidation as a way to manipulate?

5. What are the feelings you are trying to numb by your manipulative behaviors?

6. Do you ultimately feel more in control or out of control?

*Do **I** want to live each day in enjoyable energy or exhausted energy?*

***MY** choices EVERY MOMENT will decide how **I** will feel about myself each day.*

(I AM Choosing…)

Self care tool:

Practice being a **GRACIOUS** *receiver of other people's* **KINDNESS.**

(Inherent Value)

17

ACTIVELY RESTING

What does it mean to ACTIVELY REST? Do you know how to rest? I don't mean sleeping, I mean resting. Do you allow yourself time to rest? Does perfectionism discourage resting? Does guilt of not doing enough discourage resting? Does anxiety about quiet time with yourself discourage resting? Learning how to rest is an important tool for self care.

One of the activities I enjoy most is sitting close to the water at a lake house my mother owns. I simply sit and look out at the water for hours at a time. No book, no cell phone, no activity other than simply sitting and watching the water. I can sit at the water for hours and be nothing but happy. I imagine when people have seen me sitting and looking out at the water for hours, they may have thought I was bored with nothing to do. Sometimes people will come down and ask if there is anything I want to do, or invite me to some activity. It is nice to be asked and included, but my response is to say; "I am sure it looks to you like I am not doing anything, but I am actually ACTIVELY RESTING. Sitting and ENJOYING looking out at the water for several hours is an ACTUAL ACTIVITY for me. When I woke up today, my plan for the day was to sit at the water and ACTIVELY REST."

It does seem to surprise people that I was not bored with nothing to do, but was ALREADY engaged in my favorite activity of ACTIVELY RESTING. Another way I like to put this is when I am asked how I am planning to spend "MY TIME" is to say my plan is to do "A big load of nothing." Translated, this means ACTIVELY RESTING. **ACTIVELY RESTING is using MY TIME only for me.** I have wondered if I could get a job ACTIVELY RESTING because I have an innate talent for it.

People push themselves to fill every five minutes of their day, feeling guilty if they stop even for one moment to take a breath and be present. I use the activity (yes, it is an actual activity) of ACTIVELY RESTING throughout my day. Just sitting alone and noticing my breath and how I feel, even for five minutes, can make all the difference in my mood. I remind myself of the importance of resting by hanging a sign on my desk at work and at my home which reads, "MY TIME." The sign reminds me to use "MY TIME" wisely and not give "MY TIME" away. It is a reminder to take five minutes for me.

Overly responsible people might consider the activity of ACTIVELY RESTING a waste of time. "I am supposed to be achieving and accomplishing so many things" is how the voice speaks inside your head. People ask me, "Is it O.K. to take care of myself and put myself first." I state clearly it is not just O.K., you are RESPONSIBLE to take care of the life you have been given. If you do not take care of yourself, who will? Not taking time for you is not an option. It is not selfish as some might suggest, especially when you have said "NO" and they did not get what they wanted from you. You are YOUR RESPONSIBILITY.

Having no balance between activity and rest may result in the UNFORTUNATE ACHIEVEMENT of an increase in medical problems, stress, anxiety, depression, overeating and addictions of all sorts. You have ACHIEVED, but is this really what you wanted? **It is ironic that you don't see any connection between being out of balance with activity and rest, until your body notifies you in some way that it has "HAD ENOUGH."** Even when your body starts to scream with physical illness, you continue feeling guilty about taking care of yourself and resting. Depression and anxiety increase, and you **STILL** feel guilty about resting. You are emotionally and physically exhausted, yet **STILL** feel guilty about taking care of yourself and resting. Learning to be comfortable and at peace sitting with yourself, your thoughts and your feelings is an important self care skill to cultivate for maintaining a balanced life. **ACTION STEPS balanced with ACTIVELY RESTING are an energizing combination.**

1. If you feel guilty for taking time to care for yourself, is this your voice, or the tapes of others in your head?

2. Whose expectations are you living with today?

3. How does living with these thinking patterns of unrealistic and punishing expectations making you feel?

4. How do you take time to ACTIVELY REST?

5. Is taking care of yourself and doing what "fills up your tank" a waste of time?

6. Do you seek out the approval of others first, before you feel comfortable taking time for yourself?

7. Do you ever find yourself apologizing to others when you put yourself and your needs first?

MY body is no longer a battlefield for MY unresolved emotions.

MY body is NOW a place of emotional PEACE.

(Inherent Value)

Fasting = *not engaging in any addictive or compulsive behaviors to numb emotional pain.*

Fasting = *letting the **feelings** flow through you to freedom.*

*Allow the **feelings**.*

*Allow the **feeling** of the **feelings**.*

*Allow **feeling** the **feelings** to heal you.*

***Fasting** for **feelings** is* **HEALING**.

***Fasting** for **feelings** is* **FREEDOM**.

(Corrective Experience)

18

Impaired Driving

(Drinking – Drugging – Texting)

Set Your Own Standard

This chapter was written as a handout for my Driving Under the Influence Group. Below is an interactive dialogue to help you identify YOUR standards, but more importantly to HONESTLY identify if you are living up to YOUR standards. My hope is that it may encourage you or someone you love to make a different CHOICE and DECISION. Your decisions are how YOUR power is manifested in YOUR LIFE and OUR WORLD.

One way for you to better understand YOUR RISK is to identify what your personal standards are when it comes to IMPAIRED DRIVING. Most people I have worked with in the First Offender and Second Offend Driving Under the Influence groups are ADAMANT that they were safe to drive after they had been drinking-drugging on the night they were arrested. They will clearly state that they were NOT at any increased risk of being hurt or hurting others.

Human nature has a tendency to repeat behaviors that have been successful. People in the Driving Under the Influence group acknowledged they had driven drunk 10-100-500 times and arrived home safely. You may have promised yourself after a heavy night of drinking-drugging that if you could just make it home safely this ONE time, you would not take the risk again, only to REPEAT the same behavior the following weekend. Repeatedly arriving home safely can develop the DISTORTED BELIEF that you are indeed a "safe drunk driver." Unfortunately, all the PRIOR safe arrivals home will not help if on the next time you take the risk to drive while impaired, you hurt or kill an innocent person. No one would say, "Yes I did run your child over and I am so sorry, but I hope you will give me credit for all the other times I was IMPAIRED and did make it home safely."

All it takes is ONE decision to change your life. ONE decision can forever change YOUR life, the life of YOUR family, and the life of an innocent person and their family. You really may BELIEVE what you are telling yourself is true. You BELIEVE that you are not at ANY increased risk after you drink/drug/text and decide to drive; but do you really believe it? You probably are aware impaired or distracted driving of any kind is dangerous. **However, what you may be failing to realize is that YOUR choices and behaviors may not be living up to your standard.** One way to identify what your REAL standards are regarding any kind of impaired driving is to answer the following questions in the example below.

Imagine you are given the responsibility to make the best decision regarding your child, or any child you are taking care of that day. Your responsibility is to walk the child out and put him/her on the school bus. Just as the child is about to climb onto the school bus, you notice the bus driver is impaired on alcohol or drugs. The bus driver acknowledges that he/she has been drinking/ drugging but assures you your child is safe and there is no reason for concern. The bus driver tells you that he/she has only been drinking/drugging probably the SAME amount of alcohol/drugs YOU consumed the last time YOU drank/drug and drove yourself home. The school is only two miles down the road and that he/she has been doing this for years and has never been in an accident. Other people say that he/she is a safe driver even after drinking. Possibly these are similar thoughts you may have had in the past about yourself and your behavior.

To identify YOUR TRUE STANDARDS, answer the following two questions:

1. **Do you as the responsible adult in charge of making a safe decision put YOUR child on the school bus? (Yes or No)**

2. **Would you put YOUR child on the school bus if the bus driver had ONLY two beers? (Yes or No)**

Your TRUE STANDARD is the awareness you ALREADY have regarding the increased dangers of impaired/distracted driving. You know it is dangerous because more than likely, you would NOT put a child YOU love on that school bus with an impaired driver. When you are potentially on the receiving end of someone else's dangerous CHOICE, you can more easily identify the RISK. **Now, you can HONESTLY identify if YOU have been OFFERING other families the SAME safe standard you would want for YOUR family.** Perhaps you have been minimizing this reality and engaging in behavior that is contradictory to your OWN standards. You do not have to seek out the opinion of anyone else to tell you about the potential danger. **How you answered the questions for your OWN loved one is the PROOF you ALREADY know the danger.**

After answering these questions many people identify their double standard. They quickly change their earlier denials that they were not at ANY increased risk to themselves or others. They now acknowledge alcohol-drugs-texting did negatively impact their mental status and ability to perform their driving responsibilities. Often you can minimize the level of your impairment. Hopefully, you have answered the questions honestly as you can only change what you have the willingness to acknowledge. Ask yourself, am I living according to my OWN standards? Are my behaviors matching my standards (Yes or No)? If you answered "NO," it is important to look at the reasons why you were not able to HONESTLY answer "YES."

Many people who come to a Driving Under the Influence group AFTER being arrested for their first DUI have many thoughts and attitudes in common regarding drinking and driving. I thought it would never happen to me. It is only alcoholics that are the drunk drivers. My friends even say I am a safe driver; that's why they want me to drive. I've done this many times and made it home safely. It would have cost too much to take a taxi. I was only two miles from my home. I have been stopped by the police in the past and they let me go; I know I can talk my way out of it again. I hadn't had enough sleep - that is why I fell asleep behind the wheel, not because of the alcohol. Ya, I did hit that side mirror, but I missed the rest of the car. Can you relate to any of these attitudes or thinking patterns? The importance of education and looking HONESTLY at your behavior is to shine a bright light on your past history and make changes today. **The benefit of self awareness is that you NOW have the knowledge to become powerful in YOUR own life.** Now you have the ability to make different choices regarding your future behavior, BEFORE you make a decision that changes your life forever.

Set your OWN standards and work hard to live up to them in spite of negative peer pressure. **OFFER other people and their families what you would want for yourself and your family.** I am often asked the question: how much alcohol/drugs do I think is safe to drink/drug and drive. **My answer is always the same: the exact same amount of alcohol/drugs YOU would feel safe having the bus driver drink-drug prior to putting YOUR child on the school bus, and sending him/her off to school.**

1. What have you been telling yourself to rationalize engaging in a behavior you ALREADY know is dangerous?

2. What are some of the reasons you may be making decisions that do not live up to your own standards?

3. What changes will you **COMMIT** to NOW to live according to YOUR STANDARDS?

Choose

Wisely!

If you feel that you cannot have what you would like in **YOUR PRESENT DAY** because of your PAST, you are basically setting an **INTENTION** that **YOUR** life will never be what **YOU** want, so why bother trying.

This BELIEF keeps you apathetic and you struggle to motivate yourself to work on having a **CORRECTIVE EXPERIENCE** to change.

(Corrective Experience)

BEGIN

SURRENDER

DELIGHT

*My spirit **ALREADY** knows all my human life will ever need to know.*

(Internal Wisdom)

19

YOUR

INTERNAL WISDOM'S WRITING PRACTICE

I have continued my meditation and writing practice for many years, as I find it is the most effective way of contacting my INTERNAL WISDOM. My father over the years would give me INSPIRATIONAL BOOKS to read and would say, "Don't read it cover to cover - when you need some inspiration just open it to any page and read what is written." I have followed his guidance for many years. I will mark the date on a particular page I randomly opened to, as well as make notations of thoughts and feelings that come up at the time. When I look back at the pages over the years I can see how I have continued to emotionally grow, and how problems that seemed so overwhelming and unsolvable have long been resolved and forgotten. I can see in my writings how growing and learning through my own issues has impacted my current work.

I have included several of my meditation writings in the last section of the book. I have left space for you to begin writing and creating your OWN practice of hearing and documenting YOUR INTERNAL WISDOM. When you are looking for an answer/direction or simply need to feel comfort within yourself, do the following: sit quietly for a few minutes - breathe - open to any page in the book - read a saying - mark the date - quickly write what comes to mind. Don't put much thought into it. Feel the energy of your INTERNAL WISDOM - trust it - write it down. Begin creating YOUR own book over the years by continuing to add YOUR INTERNAL WISDOM to the pages. Over time you will have a collection of your own INTERNAL WISDOM to consult for direction and inspiration. You will also be able to see the progress you have made in making changes in how you are interacting in the world. Celebrate changes in your awareness of identify and challenging negative thought patterns. Replace them with YOUR new personal mantras that reflect your INHERENT VALUE and worth as a human being. Although I have written the original book, my hope is that over the months and years it will eventually be filled with **YOUR ORIGINAL WRITING** that you will one day share with others.

I am walking freely and happily in my life unrestricted. I am walking with such ease - with no effort - I am comfortable and safe in my own life. If I were meant to live in the past I would not be given a new day. Day after original writing (My Path).

You have done well Gal - left what you knew to find what you did not even know was lost. Keep at it - yes - yes I have arranged and created it all - it is your willingness that sets it all in motion. Wrote during sabbatical.

You are basing your future on what has happened in the past - feeling it can only be the same - that is why you are sad and discouraged - you think, why look forward to this day when it will be like the past? Your future is so much BRIGHTER and ALIVE (Thought Cascade).

It is not a reward in the future. LIVE NOW! PEACE NOW! JOY NOW! HAPPINESS NOW! I don't need to know what is on the path ahead in life because I know LOVE is on that path, so no matter what happens I am helped and loved. Live by what I know to be true - LOVE - not by what looks like it is true - fear (Intention).

Don't make something try to work that I have outgrown - don't be afraid to make a change - don't look back - look forward to the wonderful new opportunity - don't be afraid or angry - let it all go – yes, it is a good time. Fear of making change in my job (Corrective Experience).

Does this choice or decision offer my body-mind-soul comfort-joy-peace?

Be at peace, Gal - just be gentle - you must-must-must-must-must take care of yourself. Don't be waiting - YOU are living your eternity NOW. My thoughts can keep me in captivity or free me. Relax - you have eternity to get is all figured out - there is no rush - there is no need for regret - Live in Eternity and Be at PEACE (Thought Cascade).

Just ask ME (Internal Wisdom) and expect me to answer. How much easier can I make it for you! ASK ME - EXPECT ME - THANK ME. Your work is now done - MY Internal Wisdom's work begins.

Looking at the past is to be used only for learning - not to be relived NOW. Anytime I give something away, there is simply more given to me. I don't want to battle with fear. I just want to LIVE! As you prepare for the next leg of your journey, ALL will be well (Corrective Experience).

Wherever LIFE takes me I am ready for the change. Heal me from the bondage of waiting (Corrective Experience).

Good luck Gal - I am with you - I feel now that I can set you down as your Authentic Soul - you know who you are. Identify what your authentic soul wants. The dreams and I will arrange it all (My Path).

ALL CHANGE is simply a learning opportunity - no need to fear - every change is an opportunity to learn. I will not give away this day simply because I do not know the future. I trust my Creator's plan for my future so I ENJOY TODAY as a way to give thanks that my future is secure (Corrective Experience).

What more do you want than to wake up each day and look out through the eyes of who you were born to be. What more than this do you need? Do you not see that your only real job (joy) in life is to live each day as your authentic self. Authentic self: Joy - Happiness - Peace - Contentment - Ease (My Path).

Are you looking again at life being hard and a problem to solve instead of seeing how much enjoyment you can squeeze out of each day? I welcome all wonderful new opportunities into my life and GRATEFULLY release all control (Corrective Experience).

If I will not accept all my good - I will feel like I am not moving - not being led - alone - isolated - empty. LOVE can only lead by providing what is good. If I don't allow myself to accept ALL GOOD - my true self - even if it is a risk - then I am alone and separated from Love. When I follow my authentic self - even when it is a risk, I am following LOVE (My Path).

When you accept you are co-creating you life with ME (Internal Wisdom), you accept that YOU are responsible for your life as it is right this minute. What would the world look like if I just enjoyed my life (Emotional Maturity)?

Prosperity is in the mind and freedom. I will be shown the way to go. There is no way not to know the direction I am to take - no way to miss out as long as I look towards THE HANDS which are the way of LOVE (Internal Wisdom).

Accepting my authentic self - all my prosperity - ALLOWING all good I desire to come into my life is what leads me out of the valley - allowing - accepting - accepting the way. (Received one month into my sabbatical when fear about the future was yelling.)

Patience for future insights is necessary. Just keep enjoying and making the most of each day - be prepared to move - be prepared to love - the flow has already been set in motion high up on the top of a mountain - it is already flowing down at a faster and faster rate - it is certain of arrival - it can do no other thing.

YOUR BELIEF is all that is necessary - belief that is fueled by allowing and accepting - not fear and refusal - all these things are already available. It is only in your mind that you are blocked from letting the good into your life (Thought Cascade).

Allow the flow, within this flow is "JOY" that is connected to nothing that is yours - it is your natural state. Just try Marn it is all you can do. My father called me Marn - many voices can reach you during meditation. Marn, it is going to be all right – see it all as learning - we are alive forever - just see it all as lessons and learning (Corrective Experience).

Run your race today with MY JOY. This experience is not adversity. It is an opportunity to learn. NOTHING IS WRONG (Corrective Experience).

Saying NO to emotional numbing opens my soul to everything. Saying NO to emotional numbing allows the Universe to go to work (Emotional Maturity).

Do you feel "energy" at the prospect of going to work each day? Look at the workplace with compassionate eyes and ask can "I" bring any help. Learning to be at PEACE while you WAIT is the next task (Actively Resting).

Will you waste the next days WAITING or enjoying the beauty of today? You will choose where you need to be because you will recognize, "I can be helpful there." (I was interviewing for work after my sabbatical.)

Do I want to be free today, or do I want to be in emotional jail by holding resentments? It is up to me. If you trusted ME and MY plan for your life you would not have to be agitated today to prove that you are right. If you live the day I HAVE PLANNED for you it will be a wonderful day of peace - joy - love - forgiveness (Emotional Maturity).

I have already opened all the doors - all you need to do is walk through without fear or second guessing - BELIEVE you deserve all the good that is about to happen - You have given much so you will be given much - It is my pleasure to help and see you enjoy your life.

Open your heart to new people and experiences without fear - when I AM THE ONE opening the door it is always and only to your good (Internal Wisdom).

My belief each day is that the glass is full and overflowing because I have emptied it of what I no longer want and have made room for all positive energy to rush in. Gentleness Gal. Avoiding life is not where you will find PEACE. Expand always (I AM Choosing).

Is what I am about to do in the mind of LOVE or MY MIND OF FEAR? Is it my spiritual self or my human self that is about to make this decision? Have I paused and looked towards LOVE BEFORE I act (Emotional Maturity)?

LOVE does not get disappointed in us - LOVE just keeps loving no matter what - LOVE just keeps being love no matter what man is doing - man's bad behavior does not change LOVE - LOVE is LOVE, no matter!

Do you want LOVE'S outcome or do you want YOUR fear's outcome? Do not be afraid of your life - be grateful for the expansion of the universe - all things are possible - Listen.
Is it OK NOT to do what is my gift? YES for now, when you have BALANCE you will go back. (ActivelyResting). (Wrote two days after I quit my job and feared I had made a mistake - nine months later I did return to my work as a therapist.)

Less Space   Less Things   More Life - Gratitude for my health is an expanding, joyous energy. (Over a one year period of time I gave away 90% of everything I owned.)

You were not created to live the energy of other people - you were created to only live your own energy. I do not need anything external to change in my life to live at peace with me (My Path).

INTERNAL WISDOM, out of MY wasteland you build an oasis. You have taken my parched life and turned it into an oasis. Believing it will be better tomorrow takes the power and opportunity out of today. Explore what is good today. There is no waiting. Your ETERNITY is happening NOW. Don't miss it (Inherent Value)!

I am representing the Universe in body-mind-soul. I AM living today exactly as I AM - missing nothing. It is all possible - no really - IT IS ALL POSSIBLE (Inherent Value).

GOD does not need to change anything in me - HE just sees HIS TRUTH in me already present. What greater experience can there be than to live at the energy of God's highest gifts to me. If you could only experience yourself as the Creator of the Universe intended - can you imagine what the day would feel like (My Path)?

No matter what kind of day the wave/me is having, it remains part of the ocean/ Mother Nature (Inherent Value).

It is not about what job I have or how much stuff I have - it is about how I want to feel about me in the world - in life. How do I want to feel about me?

I am simply life force. Does your life reflect ME (Internal Wisdom) or your fears (Inherent Value)?

No one or nothing needs to change - accepting what is already here is all that is needed. Why look for proof outside of you when inside is all that matters? To be at peace with myself. Be at peace where my life is NOW, no waiting (My Path).

Your emotional issues today are all from YOUR ANGER and not saying NO (Overgiving).

Whatever exists in the Mind of THE CREATOR already exists in me because I am Creator mind expressing in the world - what will I express today: happiness - peace - love - self love - self acceptance.

It does not matter how long there has been difficulty - LOVE heals. It can all be resolved and renewed.

I won't be born again because I have never died - I have always been - back and forth - SPIRIT to human and always return to SPIRIT. DON'T RUSH. You have your eternity to figure it all out.

I AM not waiting for freedom tomorrow - I AM experiencing freedom today - each 24 hours - MY BLESSING is today. My benefit is not at the end. It is each day (Intention).

I don't need more stuff - I need to be more grateful for what I ALREADY HAVE. Today I AM not without anything. I was not created to live in yesterday or tomorrow - simply and easily be in today.

Are you looking backwards in the past for your life today? Do you see anything you want there? I am offered a lovely day if I CHOOSE to accept it (I AM Choosing).

If I try to do something else with my life other than be who I truly am, I will ALWAYS sense I am "missing something." I have been lonely for my true self. Losing the consciousness of LOVE – well, where do I go from there (My Path)?

Every breath is a blessing from the Universe because the UNIVERSE created the AIR.

It is not my place to tell other people what to do - this one behavior has caused me SO MUCH suffering. Instead, I greet my own fears with a big hug of COMPASSION (Overhelping).

I AM not going to count the days - I AM just going to be in the day - I AM just going to live in the day. None of it has been a failure - all of it has meaning when you see it through the EYES OF MY ETERNITY (Worry Habit).

EVERY time I make a CHOICE to love instead of needing to be right, INTERNAL WISDOM nods in approval. Belief in my inherent WORTH and VALUE is all that is needed (Inherent Value).

In MY storms I remain a child of the UNIVERSE. My HEALING is today, not yesterday or tomorrow. When I need to remember LOVE is with me, I simply breathe, as the air is a gift from LOVE.

What profit is there if I start to collect the energy of my fears again? Despite my fears, the Universe is still at work. JUST turning my mind back to LOVE is the immediate resolution to any problem I am faced with (Worry Habit).

What I have learned more and more is that YOU (Internal Wisdom) have arranged for it all - even when I did not know. Realizing I want to live a gentle life. Just being in a life that is MINE, get back to your life. ALONE will not accomplish what you want. The rhythm you feel NOW is the right time to move forward (Internal Wisdom).

Enjoy the day, even when you do not know what is next. This is the opposite of waiting. All is arranged. I am just giving you more time off in the beautiful sunshine. What is there to find fault with? Expand the energy of creation (Actively Resting).

JUST LOVE
Enjoy, cherish yourself
Cherish the day
Only Good to YOU

The world is a lonely, scary and not a safe place when you see it from the perspective of a fake person. I release the past and I move forward in a new day, free of the distorted thinking of the past. I have accepted God's healing of my mind. Today is a beautiful day. I AM HERE. Today I am free of my self built cage (Managing YOUR Message).

My Authentic Soul allows me to know I am always at HOME and feel at HOME, no matter what is going on outside of me. I found a way to directly communicate with MY INTERNAL WISDOM - meditation and writing. Enjoy how you see the world as you wake up each day to your true self. My journals are my art (Internal Wisdom).

Your Sabbatical = one set of hands - Internal Wisdom
Co-creating your life NOW = two sets of hands
I now live the life I was sent to live = Authentic Soul (My Path)

When I feel like I have lost, I later realize it was something that I needed to release to move on (Corrective Experience).

You were born to joy - authentic self - because you were born to ME and of ME so joy is all that is or can be possible for you (ocean/wave). I came into the world surrounded by joy - my own joy - surround myself today with my own joy - my spirits joy - and my Creator's joy because they are all the same. Simply live in the WHOLENESS now to demonstrate your faith of ALREADY being whole (Inherent Value).

Your authentic SOUL is ME (Internal Wisdom) - Every time you express your authentic SOUL, you are expressing ME - You touch ME - You are ME in the world.

Why not me!!!! BEING ME vs. waiting. Each moment offers me the gift of making a new choice. I am deserving of the life I dream of - I am free - I am free - I am free (I AM Choosing).

No matter the results of the phone call, wholeness and healing are mine! Waiting for the results of a thyroid biopsy (Worry Habit).

Man saying it is so, does not make it so. The UNIVERSE saying it is so makes it so (Overhelping).

Don't look at a whole life - just look today - just look today - love - is there love in the day - did you live each day - love you, love others, love ME - my plan FOR you is not the external stuff - it is LOVE - how much are you loving - My plan for you and all is triggered by LOVE.

MY desire in all situations is to know my Creator. My Creator is my one and only comfort, the only source of comfort I will ever need. My Creator comforts me through my emotions - when I numb my emotions, I feel no comfort - no JOY – alone. Focus keeping your emotional connection to ME (Internal Wisdom) and you will never feel alone (Internal Wisdom).

Rain in the parched places of my life and grow a garden of YOUR WILL. I am living each day in Mother Nature's Garden safe, protected, happy, loved, and at ease (My Path).

Living your life because of what someone else says or believes about YOU is dead energy.

LIVE YOUR OWN LIFE

MY PATH

Glossary

Actively Resting: Taking time ONLY for you. ACTION STEPS balanced with ACTIVELY RESTING are an energizing combination.

Corrective Experience: Emotionally experience your INHERENT VALUE by having what I like to call a "CORRECTIVE EXPERIENCE" in the present moment. The goal of a CORRECTIVE EXPERIENCE is to learn and grow NOW, by taking an ACTION STEP in OPPOSITION to your past habitual behaviors.

Emotional Manipulation: The hostile energy of emotional manipulation guarantees YOU emotional misery.

Emotional Maturity: Develops as you CONTINUALLY accept that you are responsible for the positive and negative outcomes of your decisions.

Fairness Patrol: When you are wasting your precious time ACTIVELY noticing what other people (including complete strangers) are doing wrong from a mindset of fault finding.

Managing Your Message: When you PERFORM in the world with the goal of trying to manipulate others into having a favorable opinion of you.

Overgiving: A manipulative strategy to gain love and approval from other people at great emotional cost to yourself.

Overhelping: Pointing out the faults you find in another person, and MISTAKENLY BELIEVING they are going to thank you for your efforts.

Self Created Chaos: A pattern of self sabotaging behaviors. Your motivation for creating chaos is not because it feels good, but because it feels familiar and SAFE.

Thought Cascade: A REACTIVE NEGATIVE FIRST THOUGHT to an external problem can trigger a THOUGHT CASCADE ending in an impulsive decision. One negative thought leads to another negative thought, triggering painful emotions.

Worry Habit: Sets a powerful INTENTION for what you DO NOT WANT in the future. WORRY HABIT projects negative expectation of what you fear will happen in your life, and in the lives of those you love.

.

Friends are the family I have chosen.

I would like to offer a special thanks to friends who were encouraging and supportive in the process of writing and editing this book.

Alan H
Janet H
Paul O
Ryan S
Joan P
Cecilia S
Donna H

embracetheunknown2018@gmail.com

Made in the USA
Columbia, SC
21 August 2018